pL

Henry James

PARISIAN SKETCHES

HENRY JAMES, JR.

HENRY JAMES

Parisian Sketches

LETTERS TO THE *NEW YORK TRIBUNE*

1875-1876

Edited with an Introduction by

LEON EDEL AND ILSE DUSOIR LIND

NEW YORK UNIVERSITY PRESS

Washington Square

1957

PREFACE

Henry James's Paris letters to the New York *Tribune* of almost eighty years ago have been collected in this volume for the first time. Three of the letters were reprinted by James during his lifetime, the remainder were allowed to linger in the crumbling newspaper files in the hope that they would be forgotten. In recent years extracts from those letters that were devoted to the theater were included in Allan Wade's collection of James's dramatic criticism, *The Scenic Art;* and certain passages dealing with paintings were incorporated by John L. Sweeney in his compilation of Henry James's art criticisms, *The Painter's Eye.* The majority of the letters, however, remained uncollected, and available only to those who cared to read the files or the microfilm record.

The documents contained in the appendix to this volume were copied by Ilse Dusoir Lind in 1950 during a search of the New York *Herald Tribune* archive carried out with the kind permission of Mrs. Helen Rogers Reid. They were subsequently used, with the permission of Mrs. Reid and of Mr. William James, in an article published by Professor Lind in *PMLA* (December 1951, Vol. LXVI, No. 6, 886–910) entitled "The Inadequate Vulgarity of Henry James." The editors of the present volume wish to renew their thanks to Mrs. Reid and to Mr. James for having made this material available, and to the Houghton Library and

· *v* ·

the President and Fellows of Harvard College for Dr. Edel's continued access to the James family papers.

The date of each of James's letters (in the date line) is that of the writing of the letter and was so used on publication. At the bottom of each letter we have inserted a second date, that of the issue of the *Tribune* in which the letter appeared. Certain obvious typographical errors and other misprints have been corrected.

L. E.

I. D. L.

CONTENTS

INTRODUCTION

I

In this book we have gathered together Henry James's Paris letters to the New York *Tribune* of 1875 and 1876—his only newspaper writing during half a century devoted to the art of literature. In later years he contributed a few casual pieces to the London press, but these were clearly the work of a famous man of letters invited to say a few words in an unfamiliar medium. His commitment to the *Tribune* was of quite another character: he was young, he was confident, he was energetic, he had virtually his whole career to make. Moreover, he needed money, and he seems to have reasoned that he would gain valuable experience; the narrator in one of his later tales suggests that "in picking up things" for a newspaper, a writer "would pick up life as well."

There were to be two further attempts, in the 1890's, to write a certain kind of journalism, a series of "London Letters" for *Harper's Weekly* and some "American Letters" for *Literature;* but these, in reality, called for the sort of magazine writing Henry James had done from the time of his late adolescence. The *Tribune* experience was unique not only in that it required regularity of production as the "occasional correspondent" of a big Manhattan daily, but in the consequences it was to have for certain of the novelist's later fiction.

Introduction

At the turn of the century, twenty-five years after his *Tribune* work, the heroine of one of James's tales ruefully confesses she has agreed to write some London letters for a provincial paper: "I can't do them—I don't know how, and don't want to. I do them wrong, and the people want such trash. Of course they'll sack me." All of Henry James's feelings about his newspaper experience may be discovered in these words.

As in his attempt to write for the theater, Henry James approached his *Tribune* job with mixed feelings. He wanted to succeed, but he had distinct misgivings about American newspapers and the extent to which a man of letters could work for them without compromising his art. If the United States had produced certain authoritative organs, such as the *Tribune*, it had also produced the fly-by-night sheets which Charles Dickens had satirized in *Martin Chuzzlewit*. The time was to come when Henry James himself would create "a recording slobbering sheet," *The Reverberator*, and its snooping correspondent, George Flack; or the privacy-invading Henrietta Stackpole; or the ubiquitous Matthias Pardon, for whom "everything and everyone were everyone's business." "One sketches one's age but imperfectly if one doesn't touch on that particular matter, the invasion, the impudence, and shamelessness of the newspaper and the interviewer, the devouring *publicity* of life, the extinction of all sense between public and private." Henry James was to write these words in his notebook long after his *Tribune* phase. When he turned to that newspaper originally, however, it was because he esteemed it, and because it had been esteemed in the James family. His father had been a friend of Horace Greeley during the fight for Abolition, and had sent long, unjournalistic letters from Europe during the family's wanderings abroad in the 1850's, which the paper had published. Here was precedent enough for his second son.

The novelist was to describe, forty years later, how as a small boy he was taken by his father to the *Tribune* offices, "a wonderful world indeed with strange steepnesses and machineries and noises and hurrying bare-armed, bright-eyed men, and amid the agitation clever, easy, kindly, jocular, partly undressed gentlemen (it was always July or August) some of whom I knew at home, taking it all as if it were the most natural place in the world." He remembered some of the talk, too, among the newspaper people. One man spoke of the French theater, of an actress, Madame Judith, who was going to steal the laurels from the brow of Rachel. And another told how he had just come back from Chicago; the city was but a year or two old, "with plank sidewalks when there were any, and holes and humps where there were none, and shanties where there were not big blocks, and everything where there had yesterday been nothing." James wrote: "I became aware of the Comédie. I became aware of Chicago." The newspaper was "big to me with the breath of great vague connections."

For the adult Henry James the connections were no longer vague. He was acquainted with John Hay, who had been one of Lincoln's secretaries and was now associated with the *Tribune* in various capacities that ranged from reporter to editorial writer. To him Henry first broached his idea that he might become a Paris correspondent. The newspaper had been using a Parisian chronicle written by Arsène Houssaye, a popular devotee of the arts, who had served for a time as administrator of the French national theater. He specialized in novelty and human interest; his letters retailed gossip and miscellaneous impressions. But his correspondence was written in French, and one of Hay's jobs was to translate it. Henry James's letters would have the advantage of being written directly for publication; they would, moreover, reflect an American, rather than French, point of view.

Hay had been from the first an admirer of Henry James's work. He accordingly wrote a memorandum to the *Tribune's* editor, Whitelaw Reid, informing him of the proposal and adding that James "considers the *Tribune* the only paper where business could be combined with literary ambition." He went on:

I hope you will engage him instead of Houssaye. He will write better letters than anybody—you know his wonderful style and keen observation of life and character. He has no hesitation in saying that he can beat Houssaye on his own ground, gossip and chronicle, and I agree with him. Besides, his name is almost, if not quite, equally valuable—and far more regarded by cultivated people.

Houssaye was receiving $30 for a "not very good letter" requiring translation. Hay believed Henry would "write you a much better letter and sign his name to it" for $20 or $25.

"I think exceedingly well of Henry James," Reid replied. "Go ahead and make the bargain with him." The matter was promptly settled. A memorandum of August 11, 1875, preserved in the *Tribune* letter books, says: "Henry James Jr. is engaged to do Paris letters in place of Houssaye at $20 gold, per letter, to begin about 25th October, 1875. W[hitelaw] R[eid]." It is difficult to estimate in current terms what the gold dollar was worth in the fluctuating currencies of the then-young Third Republic, freshly emerged from the Franco-Prussian War and the Commune. But we do know that its purchasing power in Paris was considerable. By writing two letters a month, Henry James would assure himself of ten gold dollars a week.

II

Henry James crossed the Atlantic that autumn as he had planned, and took up his residence at No. 29 Rue de Luxembourg. It is now known as the Rue Cambon and it runs from the grand boulevards, a short distance from the Place de la Madeleine, to the Rue de Rivoli. The story of Henry James's year in Paris has been only sketchily told; but its principal outlines are well known. The year was to throw its light far along James's literary road. He met Turgenev, whom he greatly admired, and was taken by the Russian to

Flaubert's apartment, high up in the Rue du Faubourg St. Honoré where he encountered Zola, Daudet, Edmond de Goncourt, and the as yet unpublished Maupassant. It is something to conjure with that an American writer in his early thirties, with his reputation still to be made, found himself received in the Flaubertian *cénacle* among the literary sons and grandsons of Balzac.

Elsewhere in Paris James distracted himself by frequenting the American "colony"—that little group of New World settlers which from far back has clung to the entourage of the Arc de Triomphe and other fashionable quarters of the Right Bank. He found it less easy, inevitably, to gain access to French homes; but in the few to which he was invited, he again discovered circles both literary and artistic. He settled rapidly into a pleasant routine of writing and of social life, with the Théâtre Français always at hand to entertain him when other amusements failed. Appropriately enough, the novel he chose to write, at first destined for the *Galaxy* but sold finally to William Dean Howells for the *Atlantic,* dealt with an American in Paris. If we place the story of Christopher Newman beside the letters to the *Tribune* we can reconstruct the essential outlines of Henry James's life and interests during his winter in the French capital.

A journalist looking at James's mode of life would say today that he had ample material at hand for the *Tribune.* The newspaper was not relying upon James for its French news coverage; for that it had the seasoned William H. Huntington, and for political stories it could also call upon the services of John Paul. James was free to deal with whatever struck his fancy in the Parisian scene. A contemporary correspondent would have found material enough in the smoke-filled Sunday afternoons at Flaubert's, Turgenev's apartment in the Rue de Douai, or even the quiet evenings at Auguste Laugel's, where the American writer met Ernest Renan. But James encountered these literary folk as a fellow writer and not as a journalist, and he could hardly make capital out of the advantage which he enjoyed. In one or two of his Paris letters he does indeed guardedly allude to talk in literary circles which we can recognize as originating at Flaubert's; but the allusion has been carefully depersonalized. Concerning Turgenev, whom he carefully described in his intimate letters, he was wholly silent in his dispatches destined for the public, save to allude to a portrait of him hung in the Paris Salon—a distinctly impersonal matter.

What was left for the *Tribune* once James excluded his private experiences? There remained the theaters, the art shows, the occasional book, the newspaper controversies, and the human interest of the effervescent political scene which has always—then as now—provided an endless source of color and rich debate for the initiated spectator in Paris. The truth was, however, that Henry James did not know how to exploit this material in a newspaper's columns; he ended by giving the *Tribune* largely the residue of his literary activities. And he found the writing of the letters irksome.

His correspondence with his family discloses how quickly he lost confidence in his capacity to give Whitelaw Reid what he had so bravely guaranteed. Less than two weeks after dispatching his first Paris letter the novelist wrote (on December 3, 1875) to his brother William: "I can think of nothing to put into the *Tribune:* it is quite appalling. But I suppose it will come." William replied: "Your first letter was a very good beginning, though one sees that you are to a certain extent fishing for the proper tone or level." On December 20 the novelist wrote to his father: "I have written three letters to the *Tribune*—though I'm afraid the first was a failure from excessive length and being pitched in too vague and diffuse a key." On January 11, 1876, he told his mother he was "sickened" by the headlines in his *Tribune* pieces. "I am glad my *Tribune* letters amuse you," he wrote in turn to Howells. "They are most impudently light-weighted, but that was part of the bargain." By April he was thoroughly unhappy. "The vulgarity and repulsiveness of the *Tribune*, whenever I see it, strikes me so violently that I feel tempted to stop my letter," he told his father. "But I shall not, though of late there has been a painful dearth of topics to write about. But soon comes the *Salon*." He continues to complain of the lack of subject matter. As late as August, when the chore is at an end, he talks to Reid of "the dearth of topics during the last two or three weeks of my stay in Paris," and, as will be seen, he went outside his Paris assignment to write about Chartres and his stay at Étretat, lapsing from

Parisian reportage into the familiar travel essay which came to him with tolerable ease and in which he had already proved himself. (These were the letters, the pictures of Chartres, Rouen, Étretat, which he deemed worthy later of rescuing from the newspaper files and placing between the covers of his travel book, *Portraits of Places*.)

Try as he might, Henry James could never speak in his *Tribune* letters in the journalistic voice: it was a distinct falsetto which he could not cultivate. The voice we hear always is that of the artist and the artist-critic—and one who had made all the arts his province. He had learned early that the arts are one, that the human consciousness is the prime source of the artistic process, that the act of creation calls upon the same faculties of imagination and feeling whether it finds expression in word, pigment, sound, or clay. When all else failed him, and his *Tribune* pen lagged, he lapsed into the use of his aesthetic faculties; he could also fall back on his faithful eyes, his incomparable powers of observation:

The huge towers of Notre Dame, rising with their blue-gray tone from the midst of the great mass round which the river divides, the great Arc de Triomphe answering them with equal majesty in the opposite distance, the splendid continuous line of the Louvre between, and over it all the charming coloring of Paris on certain days— the brightness, the pearly grays, the flicker of light, the good taste, as it were, of the atmosphere—all this is an entertainment which even custom does not stale.

Introduction

"Entertainment" doubtless for the mind and imagination of Henry James, but what concern, we might wonder, would a *Tribune* reader have with atmospheric "good taste"? This is the painter at work, in blue-gray, pearl gray, and flickering light, but distinctly not the journalist, and we follow him as he enters Notre Dame and listens to vespers and watches "the sounding nave grow dusky and the yellow light turn pale on the eastern clerestory." The effect is charming and the scene is beautifully imaged; indeed, we roam cheerfully through Paris on this Christmas Day of 1875 in the novelist's company picking up sights and colors, and see them framed in delicate visual pictures. But as we read, we seem almost to hear the groan of the *Tribune* copyreader who must edit the column for persons seeking in the Parisian letters what James later burlesqued as "smatter and chatter." In the same way, when we travel with the novelist to Versailles, and he is bent on writing a political piece about France's reorganized political institutions, we find him abridging his attendance

in that musty little red and gold playhouse in which the Assembly sits, for the sake of wandering about the terraces and avenues of the park. The day had that soft, humid mildness of which, in spite of the inveteracy with which you are assured here that every biting blast is "exceptional," and which consequently piles up your accumulated conviction that it is the rule—is really the keynote, the *fonds*, as they say, of the Paris winter weather.

We can indeed imagine what the copyreader might say over the double-claused sentence, the quoted "exceptional," the *fonds* of the matter! But a few sentences later the painter goes to work again:

The long, misty alleys and vistas were covered with a sort of brown and violet bloom which a painter would have loved to reproduce, but which a poor proser can only think of and sigh. As it melts away in the fringe of the gray treetops, or deepens in the recesses of the narrowing avenues, it is the most charming thing in the world. All the old Hebes and Floras and Neptunes—there are more to a square rod at Versailles than in any old garden I know, and I know, thank heaven, a great many—were exposing their sallow nudities as if in compliment to the clemency of the weather.

We have seen enough to understand what Henry James's problems were in writing these letters. It must be said, however, that if the *Tribune* reader accepted the literary tone, the unorthodox journalistic sentences, the substitution of color for fact, he found much to reward him, over and above the descriptive felicities. There is, for example, the little trip James makes to Durand-Ruel's gallery to see the exhibition of the early impressionists, although he is still too rigid in his concepts of what painting should be to appreciate the revolution that these "refused" artists are bringing about. He tours the Salon of 1876 with the patience and vigor one requires in visiting this annual French display of miles of painted canvas; Taine, Renan, Zola, Sainte-Beuve are mentioned, sometimes reviewed; we catch the novelist at a ball hearing Johann Strauss conduct his waltzes; and on a certain occasion he is present as Giuseppe Verdi leads his *Requiem* "with a certain passionate manner." We walk through the then brand-new Paris opera; we muse over the traceries and carvings of Chartres before Henry Adams has set his studious eyes upon it; or we travel down the Seine to Rouen looking at scenery, and finally we relax on the beach at Étretat to enjoy the diving display of one of the actresses of the Palais Royal.

The letters make rewarding reading if we can surrender ourselves to James's constant need to intellectualize and analyze experience. For the novelist is unable to be the simple reporter. He criticizes; he reflects; he has a great many opinions. In sculpture he prefers figures which represent "ideal beauty." The animal statuary of Barye or the Carpeaux figures are too close to reality. The nudes seem to shiver in the winter cold. In painting, extremes of realism, such as Meissonier's minutely-depicted battle of Eylau, also displease him.

The best thing, say, is a certain cuirassier, and in the cuirassier the best thing is his clothes, and in his clothes the best thing is his leather straps, and in his leather straps the best thing is the buckles. This is the kind of work you find yourself performing over the picture; you may go on indefinitely.

But he defends Decamps because "he shrinks from none of the atmospheric mysteries and complexities . . . the great charm of art is in its being a change from

life, and not a still narrower consciousness of it." He
reacts sharply to a morally ugly subject, such as the
prize picture of the spring salon of 1876—"Locusta
trying the effects of poisons before Nero." The pictures for which he professes admiration—by Flandrin,
Millet, Boldini, Decamps, Vollon, Chaplin, Munkascy
—are those which take their subject directly from life,
which give an impression, a glimpse, frame a scene:
a landscape, peasants, fisherwomen, the charm of young
womanhood painted with elegance and grace, a striking portrait of a lady in a blue dress—these are the
contemporary subjects to which he responds with
warmth. His lengthy comment on Munkascy's studio
interior, his preferred picture at the salon, is that "it
is the work of a man who stands completely outside it
and its superficial appeals." By "standing outside"
James means the capacity of the artist to detach himself from his subject, to see it aesthetically, and to have
(we can complete James's statement) "regarding its
texture and tone, a vision and a conviction" of his own.
James is affirming, at the core of his criticism in these
letters (and it applies to his reports on the dramatist's
art, and the actor's as well), the need for the artist to
impose his own imaginative order upon his selected
materials. Ultimately this affirmation will form the
subject of one of his shortest and most suggestive tales,
"The Real Thing."

And yet it strikes one as strange that an artist who
spoke of "texture and tone," of "atmospheric mysteries and complexities," should have written with such

disparagement of the Impressionists. He grasped completely their aim "to get a vivid impression of how a thing happens to look at a particular moment." Yet he invokes against them "the good old rules which decree that beauty is beauty and ugliness ugliness" and is Ruskinian in his complaint over their unwillingness, as he sees it, to concern themselves with "the idea of the beautiful." We must be careful lest we judge Henry James here in the light of our own three-quarters century familiarity with Impressionism. At the same time we must recognize with John L. Sweeney, who edited James's art criticism in *The Painter's Eye*, that in matters of painting the novelist was essentially an amateur rather than a connoisseur. He tended to display a conservatism (or at least a failure to discard old prejudices) which did not exist in his criticism of fiction. Ultimately, as his comments in *The American Scene* show, he was to modify his judgments.

He was for realism in the arts, but not a literal reality; he demanded that any picture of the real be suffused with the artist's imagination: the imagination being in itself a thing of reality which the artist can bring from within himself to the materials of his work. Indeed the finest works of fictional romance—as distinguished from fictional "reality"—were for James those which stemmed from an imagination capable of sustaining credibility even when invoking the unreal. He admires this fluid narrative quality in his letter on George Sand, and years later he was to describe his own novel of this Parisian period as "consistently, consummately

—and I would fain really make bold to say—romantic."

We can discover between the lines of these letters, written so hastily and yet so spontaneously, a wholly coherent aesthetic. We can discern also certain of James's attitudes toward France and the French, the immediate ground of his observation. He charges the French with being facile, clever, impulsive, irresponsible, superficial, as in his allusions to French lecturers and his prompt comparison of them with American lecturers such as Emerson. He finds that the French possess that "Gallic lightness" in moral matters which the Anglo-Saxon world deplores. And yet he has always a very genuine feeling for them, for the genius of their language, for the fact that they genuinely *care* for art, for their possession of tradition and history and, above all, *style*. He likes their theater even while he shrugs off Sardou's contrived plays and the perpetual adulteries of Dumas *fils*. It is all very vivid, this Parisian city, overflowing with its manifestations of life and energy, filled with its vivacities, its rituals, its depravities. His own cosmopolitanism permits him to look for values, to be aware of his American point of view, and to recognize that there are other points of view as well in this world. We can recognize his fundamental Americanism in the high seriousness of his approach to his task, his earnestness, his sense of responsibility, his need to pass judgment, to evaluate and ponder, and in his detachment from schools and groups. He takes a distinctly democratic point of view, for instance, in discussing the Catholic education controversy; he is stanchly for the French Republic even while finding himself almost wholly in the company of monarchists; and at the same time he is fearful of Republican excesses and ignorances. He conveys a sense of shock—part of it is a sop to his readers—over the representation of certain grosser realities in Zola. On the whole, however, his views are mild and constructive; one has the feeling of a man of even temper surveying life with equanimity and a fundamental faith in the high decencies and the future of civilization.

III

The history of Henry James's relations with the *Tribune* can be briefly told. If James admitted to his family in Cambridge that he was having difficulty putting his letters together, he gave no inkling of this to Whitelaw Reid. He is always his usual cool, businesslike, professional self in the correspondence with the editor. The covering letter he sent with his first dispatch explained that "this is a thing which will have to come little by little" and expressed the hope that any headline prefixed to the letter would be "as brief and simple as possible." (This accounts for the "label" type of heading which was placed on James's letters.) When later one of his columns blossomed into subheadings, James promptly wrote a four-sentence letter making a most "earnest and urgent request" that the practice "be not continued." He added: "I object to it in the strongest possible manner and I entreat and beseech you to cause it to be suppressed. The thing is in every way disagreeable to me."

Reid readily acquiesced. James was placated and continued to send Reid two letters a month with considerable punctuality. They ran from December into July. As summer drew near, Reid inquired how long James would be away from Paris and informed the novelist that "some applications have been made for Parisian correspondence, which we have denied at once, preparing to have the benefit of your service as long as we can." There was probably no special intention on the part of the editor to suggest to Henry James that substitutes for him were readily available, but the next sentence might have caused the novelist to pause. Reid told James that his letters had not aroused much talk in other journals. He added, however, "I think they have given a great deal of satisfaction to a large majority of our readers." James replied that he was glad of this but that his letters "could find an echo in the other papers I never expected." And he announced that he would be back in Paris in the autumn, quite prepared to continue his arrangement with the *Tribune*. It was at this moment, however, that Henry wrote to his father about the "vulgarity and repulsiveness" of the *Tribune* and said he felt "tempted to stop my letter." [1]

[1] In the columns of the *Tribune* during this period there are letters of praise for most of the correspondents but none for James. After Houssaye reappeared in the paper, writing a Parisian column from time to time, a group of readers wrote

What is quite clear, as we have seen from the family correspondence, was that Henry James increasingly found this task, so lightly undertaken, to be artistically if not financially unprofitable. By midsummer, when he had written nineteen letters, he could calculate that they had yielded him the tidy sum of $380 in gold, and he knew that he had been as well paid for them as anything he did for the *Nation*. He may not have been aware that he was being paid on the whole at the same rate as most of the *Tribune*'s special correspondents. But he conceivably might have argued that as a novelist with a rising reputation he was entitled to special consideration. The letter he wrote to Reid on July 25, from Normandy, gave no reasons, but quite simply suggested that he be paid half as much again for each letter. Conceivably he felt that his trial period with the paper was over and that he was now entitled to receive the same amount as had been paid his predecessor, Houssaye.

I should like to propose to you an augmentation; viz.: that, beginning with the letter I enclose, I receive *thirty*

---

to commend his work and expressed the hope he would be heard from frequently. The letters of the political correspondent, John Paul, were proclaimed "the delights of our heart" by another group. A review of American paintings by "C. C." (Clarence Cook, the newspaper's art editor) brought reader comment urging that he write a history of American painting. The only response to James was a derogatory letter published January 22, 1876, complaining that he had misjudged harshly Barye's animal sculptures.

dollars per letter. Will you be so good as to let me know whether this is agreeable to you?

Reid's reply was unexpected. Instead of agreeing to the increase, or refusing it, he offered a general evaluation of James's work for the *Tribune* and proposed a compromise. He explained that James's subjects were often "too remote from popular interests" and that it was possible to overestimate the newspaper's "literary culture." He reminded Henry that readers of newspapers were often hurried and liked brevity, variety, and topics of wide interest; they were more likely to read a letter of one column than of two. He therefore proposed that Henry James alter the character of his letters: make them shorter and more "newsy" and also less frequent, especially since a presidential election was in the offing. He was prepared, in other words, to pay the same amount for less copy. This, in Reid's economy, would represent an augmentation of the novelist's actual rate of pay while in effect involving no budgetary changes for himself. "You must not imagine," he wrote, "that any of us have failed to appreciate the admirable work you have done for us." But he added the following forthright—and quite accurate—comment: "The difficulty has sometimes been not that it [James's work] was too good, but that it was magazine rather than newspaper work."

The letter reached James at the Château de Varennes, near Montargis, where he was spending a pleasant vacation with American friends. Although it was a wholly reasonable reply, it went beyond mere negotiation of an increase and touched James's professional problems. Reid, the brilliant reporter and editor, only five years James's senior, was in reality telling the novelist that however admirable literary culture might be, it required a certain process of transformation to be acceptable in the columns of a newspaper. His concluding remark had a peculiar and painful force: freely translated it could mean only that James's work had, in fact, not been good enough as journalism. The novelist was left defenseless. He could hardly try to convince Reid that he had indeed written good journalism or that what he had written, although it was magazine work, was what the *Tribune* should take from him. So, too, the terms offered no ground for negotiation. He was to receive the same amount for less work. But this "less" involved a significant change, an invitation to be "newsy"—more informative. A literary hack, or a professional journalist, a man who fashions his career by conforming to the needs of journals which take their standards from the reading public, might be addressed in this manner and would not think twice about it; but was it fair to ask this of a literary artist who offered his style, his reputation, his high individuality? Reid's commitment as editor forced him to take the journalist's point of view. James's dedication as artist and professional man of letters determined his reaction. The pen which answered Whitelaw Reid, from the comfortable tower guest room of the Château

de Varennes, was perhaps more incisive than it had ever
been in writing for the *Tribune*.

James began mildly enough. He recognized that his
letters were considered by Reid not "the right sort of
thing for a newspaper." Indeed he said he had been expecting to hear this from the editor. He could easily
imagine that the general reader would not have time
for his letters during an election period. He was quite
prepared to grant that his writings would be more in
place in a magazine.

But I am afraid I can't assent to your proposal that I
should try and write otherwise. I know the sort of letter
you mean—it is doubtless the proper sort of thing for
the *Tribune* to have. But I can't produce it—I don't know
how and I couldn't learn how. It would cost me really
more trouble than to write as I have been doing (which
comes tolerably easy to me) and it would be poor economy
for me to try and become "newsy" and gossipy. I am too
finical a writer and I should be constantly becoming more
"literary" than is desirable. To resist this tendency would
be rowing upstream and would take much time and pains.
If my letters have been "too good" I am honestly afraid
that they are the poorest I can do, especially for the
money! I had better, therefore, suspend them altogether.
I have enjoyed writing them, however, and if the *Tribune*
has not been the better for them I hope it has not been
too much the worse. I shall doubtless have sooner or later
a discreet successor.

What had begun as a gentle answer had ended in un-
concealed anger. And James's derisive 'they are the

poorest I can do, especially for the money" suggests that Reid's carefully chosen words, intended to distinguish between the quality of James's writing and its usefulness in a newspaper, had wholly failed of effect. To tell James that his work was "too good" was also to tell him that he could not catch the pulse of the public. Reid had offered the precise criticisms which William James had repeatedly hammered at his brother: that he was too analytical, too refined, super-subtle. The intolerable irony was that all of Henry James's efforts had been directed at achieving the very objectives Reid held up for him, "brevity, variety, and topics of wide interest." He had tried to write about matters which interested him, but without the certainty that they were of interest to his audience; he had on occasion been stilted in manner when he believed himself to be natural; he had been subtle even when he thought he was being obvious. Had he not, indeed, been trying to make a sow's ear out of a silk purse?

Here the incident might be expected to close. In due course James tired of Paris and moved to London. His failure as a journalist may have contributed to his Parisian ennui. If his siege of Paris was not going well, he would lay siege to London. The British capital surrendered quickly. Within two years Henry James was a lion in Victorian society, the celebrated author of "Daisy Miller," a writer whose works were in constant demand in the magazines. The little unpleasantness with the *Tribune* had been left far behind. When the novelist revisited the United States in 1881, bringing with him his new renown as the author of *The Portrait of a Lady,* he dined with Whitelaw Reid in the latter's New York home during Christmas week; and two years later they exchanged friendly letters when Henry asked to have certain of his old *Tribune* columns copied for inclusion in one of his travel volumes.

IV

To arrive at the end of our story we must jump across twenty years of Henry James's writing fame, almost the entire period of his "middle years," to January 5, 1895. On that evening—a drizzly, unpleasant London evening—after a five-year attempt to win a place in the theater, Henry James was brought face to face with a hostile audience. His long-cherished and carefully wrought *Guy Domville,* a handsomely mounted play, was booed by a group of irritated and unmannerly theatergoers. He seemed to accept the verdict and he abandoned the drama. He wrote in his notebook: "I take up my *own* old pen again—the pen of all my old unforgettable efforts and sacred struggles." Three weeks after the ordeal of the first night, we find him writing (also in his notebook) the outline of a story —"The idea of the poor man, the artist, the man of letters, who all his life is trying if only to get a living— to do something *vulgar,* to take the measure of the huge flat foot of the public." Was there not, he asked himself, a story in that?

It is suggested to me really by all the little backward memories of one's own frustrated ambition—in particular by its having just come to me how, already twenty years ago, when I was in Paris writing letters to the N. Y. *Tribune,* Whitelaw Reid wrote to me to ask me virtually that—to make 'em baser and paltrier, to make them . . . vulgar. . . . Twenty years ago, and so it has ever been, till the other night . . . the *première* of *Guy Domville.*

Henry James's imagination played over such old and still bitter memories in one of those intimate monologues which make of his notebooks a fascinating record of the creative process. He would trace the history of "a charming little talent, charming artistic nature," the victim of the effort to "make, as it were, a sow's ear out of a silk purse."

He tries and he tries and he does what he thinks is coarsest and crudest. It's all of no use—it's always "too subtle," always too fine—never, never, vulgar enough. I had to write to Whitelaw Reid that the sort of thing I had already tried hard to do for the *Tribune* was the very worst I *could* do. I lost my place—my letters weren't wanted.

For five months the idea lay dormant, but in June 1895 James returned to it, recapitulating: "It is the old story of my letters to the N.Y.T. where I had to write to Whitelaw R. that they 'were the worst I could do for the money.' . . . I lost that work, that place. . . ." And so the tale of Ray Limbert was born, the story of "The Next Time," in which the distinguished young novelist, writing for *The Blackport*

Beacon, does "the worst he can do for the money." It was to be followed by others in the same pattern, such as "The Papers"—James's direct attack on newspaper publicity—in which the reporters also do "the worst we can for the money," and by "Broken Wings," whose heroine avows, as we have seen, that in writing for *The Blackport Banner* she is attempting something beyond her talents. The light-giving beacon, the high-flying banner, are associated in both "The Next Time" of 1895 and "Broken Wings" of 1900 with James's mythical town of Blackport—or shall we say with the black forces of a press which, beneath its avowed aim of offering public enlightenment, vulgarizes all that it touches.

The notebook entries show that James had clearly associated "my letters weren't wanted" with the play which the public had so brutally told him it didn't want. And into "The Next Time," written during 1895 and published in the *Yellow Book,* he wove his sense of being a rejected author—wrote it out with an easy cheerfulness and mocking irony which cushioned inner heartbreak. The little pathetic comedy touches the eternal problem of the artist, aware of his gifts and insights, who discovers the extent to which these serve to cut him off from an insensitive world.

As always in these fables Henry James dramatizes the situation by selecting high contrasts: there is the novelist, Ray Limbert, who wants to write a crashing best seller and succeeds in producing masterpiece after masterpiece which only a discriminating few appreciate; beside him James places the figure of a writer of endless successes—"the spoiled child of the booksellers" —who just once would like to be an "exquisite failure." Jane Highmore, the prolific lady, argues that a success is "as prosaic as a good dinner: there was nothing more to be said about it than that you had had it." Mrs. Highmore wants to treat herself, so successful has she been, to "an hour of pure glory": she would like to write a great book rather than a merely successful one. Yet each of her novels outsells its predecessor, and every work Ray Limbert writes—trying all the while to make it vulgar enough to earn him his bread and butter—ends as a glorious failure.

Thus the adequate and inadequate vulgarity are placed into the scales. For a while Limbert works for *The Blackport Beacon.* What follows Henry James reproduced from life, without the changes his imagination usually wrought in his fictions. It was as if he had just reread his correspondence with Whitelaw Reid. The *Beacon* wants "something more chatty" from Limbert, they ask him to make his columns gossipy, personal. "Why, that's just what his letters have *been!*" the narrator exclaims. But apparently Limbert hasn't stooped low enough. And he burns his bridges by echoing Henry James's oft-repeated remark—he has done the very worst he can do for the money![2]

[2] That James continued to see his relationship to journalism in this manner is further indicated in an unpublished letter

Introduction

In the remaining episodes of the story Limbert tries
to edit a magazine with the same fatal exquisiteness.
The circulation takes a plunge and he is again out on
the street, writing his unwanted novels and without the
means to support his wife and children. His serialized
The Major Key is "rather a great performance than a
great success." He dreams always that perhaps "the
next time" he will achieve the necessary vulgarity, the
vigorously sought lucrative commonplace. Meanwhile
the financial pressures bear down upon him.

Within doors and without Limbert's life was overhung by
an awful region that figured in his conversation, compre-
hensively and with unpremeditated art, as Upstairs. It
was Upstairs that the thunder gathered, that Mrs. Stan-
nace kept her accounts and her state, that Mrs. Limbert
had her babies and her headaches, that the bells for ever
jangled at the maids, that everything imperative in short
took place—everything that he had somehow, pen in hand,

---

written by him in 1897 shortly after he had ceased contrib-
uting his series of "London Letters" to *Harper's Weekly*.
To his journalist friend, W. Morton Fullerton he wrote:
"Journalism will have absolutely none of me. The Harpers
ten months ago asked me in a deluded hour for some 'London
letters' for their 'Weekly'; and I accepted, for the money,
which was considerable, and wrote some nine or ten monthly
ones. *Or,* they have just written to me, dismissing me as you
scarce would an incompetent housemaid. And yet I tried to be
so Base!—yes, yes—your man is right. Be of a platitude;
nothing else will serve. Be as empty as a vacuum and as general as an omnibus."

to meet, to deal with and dispose of, in the little room on the garden level.

But the "next time" never comes. Limbert writes himself to death, the pen falls from his fingers without his ever having achieved a modicum of the popularity he needed in order to live; and Jane Highmore goes her way still hoping for her "next time," when she will write something that will be ignored by the multitude and praised by the few. For her, too, the "next time" will never come.

V

Today, almost a century after James's letters were written to the *Tribune*, they may be read not so much for the ephemeral things they chronicled as for the picture they offer us of a sensitive and discriminating American, an American of large imagination, sauntering through the very French scenes to which thousands of his countrymen continue to flock. They can be read equally for their vivid and lively prose; they stem, after all, from the same fertile pen which wrote the novels, the criticism, the autobiographies. The Parisian sketches may be too literary, too reflective, as journalism, but they possess intelligence and suavity, they speak for good manners, refined taste, high civilization. The letters, and the stories which were an outcome of them, raise certain fundamental issues: the function of responsible journalism, the danger to privacy resulting from certain newspaper conditions and the depravity of public taste; the danger—James was prophetic

—of the reporter who, under the banner of "freedom of the press," considers himself free to peep through every keyhole. In creating George Flack, James predicted a now all-too-familiar type. In inventing *The Reverberator*, he not only documented for posterity a certain kind of scandal sheet of his time, but foresaw the advent of the twentieth-century tabloid. And in his late stories of frustrated and misunderstood authors— "The Death of the Lion," "The Next Time," "The Figure in the Carpet"—he expressed much more than his personal feeling that the finest things in art suffer for want of fine appreciation. He seemed indeed to foresee that the artists of our century would be under pressures similar to those which weighed on Limbert—pressures of the mass media asking the creative mind to substitute the obvious for the subtle, the coarse for the fine, the cliché for original utterance. In this way he made universal what had been a private experience: converted it into an artist's creed proclaiming the sovereignty of style, the sacred uniqueness of the creative consciousness.

LEON EDEL
ILSE DUSOIR LIND

New York University

PARISIAN SKETCHES

PARIS REVISITED

Letter from Henry James, Jr.

THE PHILOSOPHY OF LIFE IN PARIS—THE AMERICAN
QUARTER—THE NEW PLAY BY ALEXANDRE DUMAS—
THE OPERA—ROSSI IN "KEAN"

[FROM A REGULAR CORRESPONDENT OF THE "TRIBUNE"]

PARIS, Nov. 22.—I have often thought that some
very entertaining remarks might be made under the
title of "Paris Revisited"—remarks that would find an
echo in many an American heart. The American who
comes to Paris for the first time receives, of course, a
multitude of agreeable impressions; he takes to the
French capital, generally speaking, as a duck to water,
and he is not slow in maturing his opportunities for
diversion. But no American, certainly, since Americans
were, has come to Paris but once, and it is when he returns, hungrily, inevitably, fatally, that his sense of
Parisian things becomes supremely acute. In the interval it may have faded and faltered, and tempted him
to fancy that distance was lending enchantment and
memory playing him a trick. Was it really so very
good as all that? Were the dinners at—wherever you

Notes begin on page two hundred and twenty-nine.

choose—so unfathomably to the purpose; were the shop
fronts in the Rue de la Paix so picturesquely irresistible;
was there in the acting of Céline Chaumont [1] so infinite
a titillation? Our friend comes back with a standard,
with an ideal, and it is now his pleasure to see whether
the city of his predilection will keep her promises. It is
safe to say that, as a general thing, she does, and that
at those points where she is really strong she wears well.
You may not like Paris, and if you are not extremely
fond of her you will in all probability detest and abomi-
nate her. I have known admirable cases of both states
of mind, and the height of my ambition is to do impartial justice to each. But even if you don't like her
you must at any rate admit that there are certain
matters that she understands to perfection, and that if,
from necessity or from choice, one allows these things
to play a large part in his life, one inevitably comes to
think that the problem of existence is solved more com-
fortably here than elsewhere. The French have always
flattered themselves that they have gone further in the
art of living, in what they call *l'entente de la vie*, than
any other people, and with certain restrictions the claim
is just. So far as a man lives in his senses and his tastes,
he certainly lives as well here as he can imagine doing;
and so far as he lives by the short run, as it were, rather
than by the long, he is equally well off. They seem to
me to understand the "long run" much better in England. There, if you live by the year, or by the semi-
decade, say, you are free to find yourself at all points
in relation with the world's best things. But the merit

of Paris is that you have not to look so far ahead, and that without heavy machinery, by the day, by the month, by the season, you are surpassingly comfortable. There is to be found here, in other words, a greater amount of current well-being than elsewhere. And if I spoke just now of a gentleman's senses and tastes, it is that they are certainly a very respectable class of phenomena. We most of us transact our moral and spiritual affairs in our own country, and it is not cynical to say that for most of us the transaction is rather rapidly conducted. We wander about Europe on a sensuous and esthetic basis—eating good dinners, rolling over smooth roads, served by sympathetic domestics, staring at picturesque scenery, listening to superior music, watching accomplished acting. We have all our private joys and miseries, which demand a greater or less amount of attention; but the average American in Europe, traveler or resident, makes up the substance of his life out of these things. Whether he might not do better is a question I am not discussing; certain it is that these things are offered him in Paris in a fashion which enables him to lay down his money with one hand and take with the other in perfect security. His security puts him in good humor, and though he has decidedly to lay down more money each year than the last, he finds nothing to break the charm, and mutilates an axiom which he considers philosophic, to the effect that it is better to pay much for delights than for disappointments.

This autumnal season, which is just coming to a

close, is the time at which this appreciative alien may be chiefly observed at his devotions. The numerous Americans who have been spending the summer in Europe congregate doubly during September and October upon the classic region, about a square mile in extent, which is bounded on the south by the Rue de Rivoli and on the north by the Rue Scribe, and of which the most sacred spot is the corner of the Boulevard des Capucines, which basks in the smile of the Grand Hotel. The ladies, week after week, are treading the devious ways of the great shops—the Bon Marché, the Louvre, the Compagnie Lyonnaise; the gentlemen are treading other ways, sometimes also, doubtless, a trifle devious. It has seemed to me, however, this year, that our compatriots are decidedly less numerous than usual, and that on a walk from the new Opera [2] to the Palais Royal one really hears almost as much French as American. The explanation of the mystery, of course, is in the fact that people at home "feel poorer," but the American idiom is dear to Parisian ears, and the sorrows of Wall Street find an echo on the boulevards.[3] I don't mean by this, of course, that the shops are perceptibly shabby. Paris seems more than ever, superficially, a vast fancy bazaar, a huge city of shop fronts. But it may at least be hoped that if the autumnal scramble for petticoats has been less frantic than usual, there have been, in compensation, fewer cases of smiling perjury over the counters and of hope deferred at the hotels.

Parisian affairs proper are just now rather quiet, and there is nothing very noticeable going on. The winter, and what for good or for ill the winter brings with it, has hardly begun. When I speak of Paris I do not include Versailles, where, as you know, the Assembly has for some time been in session, busily arranging the manner of its own demise, or rather of its resurrection.[4] The new electoral law has been exhaustively discussed, and it would seem that there is nothing left but to put it manfully into practice. When this has been peaceably and regularly done, and a new Assembly is lawfully installed, the largest step yet will have been taken toward making the Republic seem a permanently reasonable and comfortable state of things. In Paris the first symptoms of the winter are to be looked for at the theaters. Most of them are bringing out at this time the pieces which they expect to carry them through the next six months—or through as many of them as may be. The Français, as yet, has given only promises; but its promises cast the performances of the others in the shade. The Théâtre Français has in rehearsal a piece by the younger Dumas,[5] and this constitutes, from the Parisian point of view, a very great event. A *coup d'état* by Marshal MacMahon, an invasion of France by Prussia—it would take something of that sort to equal it. M. Dumas is a great favorite with the *Figaro* newspaper, and the *Figaro*'s compliments—which is saying a great deal—are almost as ingenious as its abuse.[6] Either in good humor or in bad it is, to my sense, a most detestable sheet; but it certainly understands in perfection the art of advertising a man. It has kindled a crackling fire under the *Étrangère*, and it will keep the pot boiling until the play is produced. The greater part of the *Figaro*, the other day, was taken up with an article of many columns about the reading of the play to the actors. Of course the papers could say very little that was definite, for the subject was not to be deflowered. But everything that talking without telling could do the *Figaro* achieved; it even gave the names of the characters—a piece of information which, for Dumas' regular admirers, leaves infinite pasture for the imagination. The French have a particular word for this sort of literary service; they call it to *soigner* an artist or his work—to take care of them. *L'Étrangère* is being very well taken care of. Victorien Sardou [7] has hitherto been supposed, I believe, to enjoy the supreme good fortune in the way of having his plays talked about, and even quarreled about, beforehand. But I believe Sardou has been accused of pulling the wires himself, and this Alexandre Dumas neither needs nor would condescend to do. Sardou, however, has just produced very quietly at the Gymnase a long serio-comic drama which is pronounced good, but not good for Sardou. There would some day be something interesting to say about this supremely skillful contriver and arranger—a man who, as one may phrase it, has more of the light and less of the heat of cleverness than anyone else; and if *Ferréol* is still being played when the day comes round, it will serve as a text.

The new Opera is open, and to all appearance very prosperous. There were many prophecies, I believe, that so elaborate an establishment could never be a paying enterprise, but the present fortune of the Opera seems to be very positively confuting them. The winter has not begun, the class of people who keep their opera box as they keep their coupé has not returned to Paris, and yet the magnificent house is magnificently full. On the other hand, this is a season when strangers and provincials are numerous, and everyone has to go at least once to see the house. When the house has been seen it may be less crowded. The new Opera has been for any time these six years the most obvious architectural phenomenon in Paris, and this may seem rather a late day for speaking of it; but now that the whole great edifice stands complete, and that the regime that produced it has crumbled away around it, it has a sort of significance and dignity which were not down in the program. The Opera is already a historical monument; it resumes in visible, sensible shape what the Empire proposed to itself to be, and it forms a kind of symbol —a very favorable one—of the Empire's legacy to France. There may be differences of opinion about the beauty of the building; to my sense it is in a high degree picturesque and effective, but it is not beautiful; but no one can deny that it is superbly characteristic; that it savors of its time; that it tells the story of the society that produced it. If this, as some people think, is the prime duty of a great building, the Opera is an incomparable success. It seems to me that a noble edifice should say something *to* a community as well as of it, and that unless, in both ways, it can speak agreeably, it had better hold its tongue. The outside of the

Opera is, I repeat, however, an old story; it is only the
great golden *salle* itself that is a current question. If
France is down in the world just now, there is something fine in seeing her make her protest, recover her
balance, where and how she can. It does it along a certain line just now at the Opera, where they are giving
the *Hamlet* of Ambroise Thomas, with Mme. Carvalho
and Faure.[8] It is the French genius alone that pays
the cost of the spectacle—French architecture, French
painting, French music, French singers, and certainly,
in spite of Shakespeare, a French libretto. Ophelia, in
her madness, comes forth and delivers her rue and rose-
mary to the *corps de ballet*. M. Thomas' music is ponderous and monotonous, but nobler singing and acting
than Faure's and more artistic vocalization than Mme.
Carvalho's it would be impossible to find. The house
is perhaps a trifle disappointing—a trifle less fabulous
and tremendous than one was encouraged to suppose
it. Reasonably viewed, it is superb and uninteresting.
It is nothing but gold—gold upon gold; it has been
gilded till it is dark with gold. This is doubtless, from
the picturesque point of view, rather a fine effect for
a theater to produce. The really strong points at the
Opera are the staircase and the *foyer*. The staircase is
light and brilliant, though I think a trifle vulgar; an
immense affair of white marble, overlaid with pale
agates and alabasters, climbing in divergent arms and
crowned with a garish fresco of nymphs and muses, in
imitation (of all people in the world) of Luca Giordano.[9] If the world were ever reduced to the dominion

of a single gorgeous potentate, the *foyer* would do very
well for his throne room. It is a most magnificent apartment, and, like the auditorium, gilded all over a foot
thick—a long golden corridor whose only reproach is
that it leads nowhere. It could lead to nothing grander
than itself. In the faraway ceiling, dimly and imperfectly through the dusky glow of gas and gilding, you
make out the great series of frescoes by M. Baudry.[10]
They are very noble and beautiful, and the most interesting things in the building. You manage to perceive
that much of this is exquisite, and you cannot help
feeling a certain admiration for a building which can
afford to consign such costly work to the reign of cob-
webs.

A month ago the shopwindows in New York were
filled with portraits of Ernesto Rossi, the Italian tragedian,[11] who was coming over to tread in the deep foot-
prints of Salvini—or as he hoped, I suppose, to make
new ones of his own. You will have perceived by this
time that he has not arrived, though you may but imperfectly appreciate his motives for breaking his engagement. He is having a quite extraordinary success
in Paris, and he remembers the adage about a bird in
the hand. On his way to embark for America he
stopped a night in Paris to play and the next morning he found himself famous. I am very sure that
his great part, *Kean*, would not have encountered in
America the prosperity it enjoys here, where it has
been played steadily for the last two weeks—a great
triumph for a drama in a foreign tongue. *Kean* is

the late Edmund Kean, the English tragedian, as portrayed by the late Alexandre Dumas. The part was created by Frédéric Lemaître, and was one of his most extraordinary achievements.[12] I listened to Rossi the other night in company with an old gentleman of a retrospective turn, who would let nothing pass without assuring me that "Frederick" did it fifty times better. But in spite of my neighbor I enjoyed Rossi—in spite of my neighbor and in spite of *Kean*. The play is the most fantastic farrago of high-spirited nonsense that even the impudent imagination of Alexandre Dumas could offer as a picture of "insular" manners. The first three quarters of the piece are mortally dull (in the Italian version), and Rossi is remarkable but not exciting. But toward the end of the fourth act poor Edmund Kean is represented as refusing to act his part because he is in a passion of jealousy of George IV, who is making love to his mistress. He rages up and down his dressing room, and declines to go on, though manager and prompter and dresser are all on their knees to him. At last George IV comes in, and joins in the suppliant chorus, but Kean laughs in his face, and still keeps the house waiting. At last he is reminded that the performance is for the benefit of a crippled clown, who was his comrade in the days when he made his living by turning somersaults at fairs, and at this hint he collapses, wraps himself in the mantle of Hamlet, and plunges into his part. In the next scene we see him on the stage consorting with Ophelia, and feverishly watching George IV in the house. This scene is brief and rapid, but it is admirably played, and it decides in a moment the actor's success. Kean, consumed with jealousy, sees George IV enter the box of the woman he loves, and from this moment he is less and less in his part and more and more certain to fling it aside and betray himself. At last he does so in a magnificently grotesque explosion of wrath at the Prince and sarcastic abuse of himself—tumbler, clown, vile histrion, Punchinello! He rushes to the footlights and pours out a volley of delirious bravado. "Punchinello? —so be it!" he cries, and he shoulders his princely sword, like Punch's stick, and executes a sort of furious mocking dance. It is horribly and yet most effectively fantastic, and it makes nearly all the tumult in the theater that the real scene might have made. Rossi will doubtless do this quite as well in America, if he ever gets there; but will it be as highly relished? I doubt it. The Paris theater-going public seizes an artist's intention with extraordinary alertness.

HENRY JAMES, JR.
December 11, 1875

2

PARIS AS IT IS

Letter from Henry James, Jr.

THE EXHIBITION OF BARYE'S ANIMAL STATUARY—THE
STORY OF THE SCULPTOR'S CAREER—HIS TRIUMPH OVER
DIFFICULTIES—EXCELLENCE OF HIS FIGURES—CAR-
PEAUX'S GROUPS AND BUSTS—THE DECORATIONS OF THE
ODÉON THEATER

[FROM A REGULAR CORRESPONDENT OF THE "TRIBUNE"]

———————◆———————

PARIS, Dec. 6.—It seldom happens in Paris that
there is absolutely nothing taking place in the way of
an exhibition of pictures or of sculpture, though of
course the interest of the proffered works is not on
every occasion of the highest order. Ten days ago was
opened an exhibition to which the clever gentlemen
who do the *feuilletons* in the daily papers have all been
paying their compliments—a collection of the bronzes
of the sculptor Barye, who died last spring at seventy-
nine years of age.[1] Barye was a specialist—he produced
little else than wild beasts, in attitudes more or less
ferocious and voracious. But in this line he was a man
of genius, and his lions and tigers have an extraordinary reality. They are familiar half the world over,

· *14* ·

for he worked chiefly for the trade, and his models
were numerously reproduced on a small scale. To have
on one's mantel-shelf or one's library table one of
Barye's businesslike little lions diving into the entrails
of a jackal, or one of his consummate leopards licking
his fangs over a lacerated kid, has long been considered
the mark, I will not say of a refined, but at least of an
enterprising taste. Barye's early career was unsuccessful; year after year he knocked in vain at the door of
the Salon. His youth was spent in composing ineffec-
tual Cains and Abels, Josephs and Jacobs; and it was
not till he was nearly forty that he struck his vein. In
1833 he exhibited his famous "Lion at Rest," and began his fortune. Thus for the first time the unclean,
prowling, muscular beast of the jungles and deserts
made his entrance into sculpture; realism had begun
for everything else, and it was time it should begin for
him. The treatment of animals, in statuary, had always
been a compromise—especially as regards the nobler
ones. They had always been more or less chimerical and
decorative, and the lion, in particular, had figured as
a sort of ingenious compound of the sphinx and the
poodle. But Barye came to his rescue with a good will
not inferior to that of Bottom the Weaver, in the play;
he learned his secrets and represented him in all his
majesty, but in all his gluttony too. In his later years
the sculptor was appointed Professor of Drawing in the
Museum of Natural History, and the Jardin des
Plantes was allotted to him as his field of study and of
demonstration. The Jardin des Plantes was his Africa

and his Asia. Though he spent half his life in modeling wild beasts, he was a Parisian of Parisians, and he never had the curiosity or the energy to take a look at the veritable East. He perhaps felt the force of that truth (which is by no means the paradox it seems) that for artistic purposes there is such a thing as knowing too much about your subject. There are doubtless many matters in regard to which a little knowledge is a dangerous thing; but I should say that often, for the artist, it is a great knowledge that is dangerous—in the sense that it crowds out inspiration and imagination. When a writer or a painter says in answer to a request to make a sketch of a certain place or person, "Oh! I can't; I have been there too long; I have seen him too often!" he is talking purer reason than he may get credit for. But this idea with regard to Barye is quite hypothetical, and it is certain that, within his chosen opportunities, he was a diligent and profound observer. He spent most of his time at the Jardin des Plantes, and lived in as familiar intercourse with his tawny models as the intervention of an iron railing would allow. When he wanted a background of wilderness he looked for it in the forest of Fontainebleau. He was a painter as well as a sculptor, and the walls of the exhibition of the École des Beaux Arts are covered with small pictures from his hand, in oils and water colors, representing lions, tigers, and elephants, in the occasional grotesqueness of a state of nature. Some of them are lying on their backs, kicking up their heels. The landscape in these paintings, which are surprisingly humorous, is

always the oaks and bushes, the mossy glades and granite boulders of Fontainebleau. Barye had never come
before the world as a painter, and his brush does not
strike us as a particularly accomplished one. His color
is muddy, and his outline (singular to say, in a sculptor) indefinite. That his amateurish attempts with the
brush should have been deemed worthy of such exhaus-
tive exhibition, and that they should have been so seriously noticed by the critics, proves what a standing
fund of curiosity there is in Paris upon all artistic
matters. For the rest, I confess, as well, the exhibition
slightly disappointed me. It is held in the great dusky
public hall of the École des Beaux Arts, which opens
upon the Seine, and the temperature and atmosphere
of this place, on these sleety December days, are not
conducive to dreamy contemplation. Barye's works,
with very few exceptions, are small, and, in the imperfect light, require a very close inspection. It must be
added that they generally repay it. He had caught in
perfection the expression of the more formidable members of the feline race, and he renders it with incomparable certainty and vigor. He has represented them
in every possible attitude and manifestation of their
passions, and it is always the living, growling creature
that we see, with its infinite resources of sinuosity and
strength. As you look at these little bronzes of Barye,
so full as they are of compressed movement and science,
they seem to expand to the size of nature, and your eye
follows the beautiful lines of spine and muscle, and
loses itself in the softer places of the hide, as if the little

scratches were real stripes and spots, and the fractions of inches were feet. Everything in these creatures is admirable—the moving, palpable curve of back and tail, the strong, soft footfall, the irresistible sense of the perfect mechanism within. But the best thing is the heads and faces. Barye studied the leonine countenance until it had no secrets for him, and he modeled it in all its beautiful hideousness. Some of his animals, throwing back their heads from the carcass in their paws, while they swallow a peculiarly tender morsel, have an extraordinary truth to nature; you seem to see the flattening of the head, and the softening and contraction of the yellow eyes, and to hear the comfortable snarl and gurgle of the throat. Nothing in this way was too difficult for Barye to attempt; like all real masters he relished difficulties, he loved them, and he triumphantly solved the problem of impossible attitudes and inconceivable combinations. One of his works is in this respect prodigious; the "Combat of the Centaur and the Lapitha" is, perhaps, indeed, the strongest of his productions. The Lapitha is astride of the Centaur's back, locking his flanks in his powerful knees, swinging a club in his uplifted arm. The Centaur's torso is twisted back with an admirable play of muscle, and he is fiercely trying to unseat his enemy. The subject is magnificent, and the author has handled the human element in it with a skill which, for him, is quite exceptional. His men and women, of whom there are several specimens, are rather gross and unshaped; all his delicacy, generally speaking, is in his wild beasts. But here the man is as good as the horse, and the monstrous rage of the creature who finds that the combined resources of both man and horse are helpless to assist him has a really tragic expression. Though Barye was weak, outside of his animals, he had once a conception which, if he had been permitted to execute it, might have proved sublime. It would have drawn half its sublimity, indeed, from animal beauty. While the decoration of the Arc de Triomphe was still unfinished (in 1840), it was suggested to Barye to execute a group to be placed on the summit. He proposed a gigantic eagle, of 70 feet from wing to wing, lighting upon a colossal aggregation of captured towns and trophies—the eagle of victory perched upon the spoils of conquest. I don't know how it would have looked, but it sounds very fine. The plan was not carried out, as it was thought rather impertinent to the "conquered" nations—whichever, in 1840, they were. One thing more to be noticed is that the exhibition at the École des Beaux Arts is (as I have seen it well observed) an elaborate representation of cruelty. All Barye's animals—or almost all—are tearing something to pieces, devouring, fighting, weltering in blood. "The works of M. Barye, or the plastic beauty of ferocity"—that would have been a good name for the collection. If I had known nothing of its history, and had been asked to what period of art these beautiful little bronzes belonged, I should have said that they were made to amuse the ladies and gentlemen of the later Roman empire, when they wished, in their houses, a little memento of the entertainments of the circus.

France lost a few weeks since another eminent sculptor, whose funeral has just taken place at his native city of Valenciennes after a rather ungraceful delay, produced by the conflicting claims of his fellow citizens and of his widow, from whom he had been separated, and who is accused of having unduly neglected him during the last months of his life. Carpeaux was made famous by the extraordinary group of "La Danse," which he contributed to the decoration of the new Opera.[2] Every visitor to Paris has gazed at it in mingled admiration and perplexity, and it is a work which, so long as it stands there, will be sure to have gazers enough. If the whole building is characteristic of its time and place, Carpeaux's group is its most characteristic feature. An exhibition of his works is, I believe, already projected, and when it takes place I will speak of him more fully. He had immense talent, and if to seize and imprison in clay or marble the look of life and motion is the finest part of an artist's skill, he was a very great artist. The shopwindows just now are full of reproductions of his figures and busts. They are the most modern things in all sculpture. That undressed lady and gentleman who, as distinguished from the unconsciously naked heroes and heroines of Greek art, are the subjects of modern sculpture, have reached in Carpeaux's hands their most curious development. In this vicious winter weather of Paris, behind their clear glass plates, they make the passer shiver; their poor, lean, individualized bodies are pitifully real. And to make the matter worse, they are always smiling—smiling

that fixed, painful smile of hilarious statues. The smile
in marble was Carpeaux's specialty. Those who have
seen it have not forgotten the magnificent tipsy laugh
of the figures in the dancing group on the front of the
Opera; you seem to hear it, as you pass, above the up-
roar of the street.

I may allude, while speaking of such matters, to a
species of exhibition which has just taken place at the
Odéon Theater [3]—"*l'honnête et maussade Odéon*"—
the respectable and dingy playhouse of the Latin quarter. The dinginess of the Odéon has passed away; the
theater has been closed all the autumn for repairs and
embellishments. The other day it opened for the winter,
and the embellishments were found to include a foyer,
decorated with histrionic portraits and literary busts.
Several of these works are by distinguished hands, and
the theater for the last fortnight has been drawing
crowds for the sake of its entr'actes. There is of course
nothing so fine as Houdon's magnificent statue of Voltaire,[4] which thrones in the foyer of the Théâtre Français; but there are three or four interesting pieces.
Among the paintings there is a very fine portrait of
Geffroy, as Don Sallust, in Victor Hugo's *Ruy Blas*,
by Carolus-Duran, the author of that admirably rich
and simple portrait of the lady drawing off her glove,
which has lately been placed in the gallery of the Luxembourg. Carolus-Duran is of all the modern emulators
of Velasquez decidedly the most successful. His analogy
with the great Spaniard—his blacks and grays, and
gravity of tone—seems not, as they say of tomatoes, an

"acquired taste," but a natural sympathy. Among the busts there is a very fine Victor Hugo, by Schönewerk —a trifle too *sombre et fatal* but bringing out strongly the extremely handsome character of his head. Then there is an Alexandre Dumas the elder, by Chapu, which is simply superb. It breathes and speaks. That monstrous mixture of the Parisian and the African which characterized his face is most vividly rendered. It is a pity such a bust should have a name; it ought to stand there always, as a symbolic image of clever impudence. The head of Madame Sand, by Carrier, is less successful. She is muffled in a Spanish mantilla, of which the lace is very elaborately wrought; but the meager, imposing little visage surely does not belong to the very positive author of *Lélia* and *Consuelo*.

Mademoiselle Déjazet [5] has just died, and 150,000 people have followed her to the grave. She was seventy-eight years of age, and she had acted almost uninterruptedly from her fifth to her seventy-seventh year. It was in its way a stupendous career. When she was a child she played the parts of old women, and as a septuagenarian she represented giddy lads and lasses. She has had the funeral of a crowned head; there could not be a better example of the ingrained Parisian passion for all things theatrical than this enormous manifestation of homage to the memory of a little old lady who was solely remarkable for the assurance with which she wore trousers and sang free-and-easy songs.

HENRY JAMES, JR.
December 25, 1875

3

VERSAILLES AS IT IS

Letter from Henry James, Jr.

THE ELECTION OF SENATORS—ALTERED ASPECT OF VER-
SAILLES—PICTURESQUENESS OF THE PLACE—THE PROS-
PECTS OF THE REPUBLIC—M. TAINE'S NEW BOOK—
GLIMPSES OF THE OLD REGIME

[FROM A REGULAR CORRESPONDENT OF THE "TRIBUNE"]

———— ◆ ————

PARIS, Dec. 16.—There is only one thing talked
about just now in Paris—the election of the 75 permanent senators.[1] The elective process has been going
on for upward of a week, and turning out an average
of 10 names a day; a day or two more will complete
the list. In the evening, on the boulevards, at the
theaters, in the cafés, the *Soir*, the paper which comes
out at nine o'clock, is pounced upon with extraordinary
avidity. You will some time since have received full
news of the reiterated, and in its effect really very dramatic, victory of the Left, and I have moreover no
warrant to examine the political aspect of the question.
But such questions have in Europe, more than with us,
a picturesque aspect as well, and of this latter, in the
present case, I had a glimpse the other day, which I

found sufficiently entertaining. It was the first day of the voting for the senators at the Assembly; and I repaired to Versailles, invoking as discreetly as a foreigner may in such a matter, good fortune upon the Republican councils. It is very possible that the proceedings in the Assembly might not have been found especially striking by an observer who insists always on very novel and acute sensations; but certainly, taking one thing with another, I deemed my afternoon decidedly remunerative. There is entertainment enough, of a mild, misty winter day, in strolling about that stately solitude of Versailles. Now that the French legislative body is permanently established there—the new Senate Chamber has just been constructed, with extraordinary celerity—the melancholy of the place is a little less intolerable than formerly, and you may go and enjoy its fine historic flavor with comfortable equanimity. I have just been reading the first installment of the new work by M. Taine,[2] lately so attentively expected—*Les Origines de la France Contemporaine*—in which he sets forth with his usual vividness and vigor the prodigious wastefulness of the manners and customs introduced by Louis XIV. His pompous architecture swallowed up millions of treasure, but in view of the excellent use to which it is now being put we may almost absolve him. Versailles seems to have been made on purpose to offer a haven of security to a Parliament situated as the French Assembly is—a Parliament for which the "emotional" character of the population renders the national capital an unsafe abode. Its stillness

and spaciousness, its air of decency and dignity, all
seem a guarantee of undisturbed deliberations. It had
never appeared to me before to have so much of this
drowsy majesty. I had always been there in summer,
when the fountains were playing, the avenues green,
and the long polished floors of the gilded halls dotted
with Paris holiday-takers or American tourists—looking like flies on horizontal mirrors. But all deserted
palaces and gardens should be seen in the chill and
leafless season. Then nature seems to give them up to
your sympathy and they appear to take you into their
confidence. I abridged my attendance in that musty
little red and gold playhouse in which the Assembly
sits, for the sake of wandering about the terraces and
avenues of the park. The day had that soft, humid
mildness of which, in spite of the inveteracy with which
you are assured here that every biting blast is "exceptional," and which consequently piles up your accumulated conviction that it is the rule—is really the
keynote, the *fonds*, as they say, of the Paris winter
weather. The long, misty alleys and vistas were covered with a sort of brown and violet bloom which a
painter would have loved to reproduce, but which a
poor proser can only think of and sigh. As it melts
away in the fringe of the gray treetops, or deepens in
the recesses of the narrowing avenues, it is the most
charming thing in the world. All the old Hebes and
Floras and Neptunes—there are more to a square rod
at Versailles than in any old garden I know, and I know,
thank heaven, a great many—were exposing their sal-

low nudities as if in compliment to the clemency of the weather. There is nowhere else, surely, such a redundancy of more or less chiseled marble; it is a forest of statues, as well as of trees. My only complaint against this moldy mythology, however, is that it is kept in a trifle too good repair; like everything else in France, it is carefully *administré*. There are none of those absent arms and diminished bosoms which are so abundant in Italy, and which seem to place one in communication with those departed generations in recovery of whose familiar caresses one may fancy them to have crumbled away. On one of the great shallow basins of the fountains a handful of people were trying to skate on some very sloppy ice; everyone, I noticed, was in the primary stages of skill. If there is any amusement, however abortive, to be picked up here, it is wonderful how many persons seem to have been eagerly waiting for it. I was surprised, nevertheless, at the skaters at Versailles floundering about so gracefully. To learn to skate requires, of all things, continuity of practice, and that must be rare where the winter is, according to an excellent expression, not "frank." In some of the great avenues, where the clumsy old coaches of the Bourbons used to roll, the little red-legged soldiers of the present Republic were learning their manual. Their corporals were at them, and smiting their muskets into the proper attitudes; but in spite of all the ugly things that lie behind it, the spectacle looked cheerful enough in the watery sunshine. Here and there, in open places, a couple of panting conscripts were learning to do the bugle call. The bugleman was marching them off their legs and giving them "patterns" to copy by, like the flourishes of a writing master. The poor fellows were stumping along under his nose, purple in the face with their exertions, and their repetition of the airs he had given had, indeed, as many square corners as a schoolboy's flourishes. But in the soft, impartial echo that melted away through the park, it seemed to me that their notes sounded as well as his own.

One regards the present Assembly with an increase of interest now that it is about to become historical. As I looked down upon the 500 not particularly handsome or individually impressive gentlemen who were chatting and edging their way about in the pit of the little rococo theater, it was impossible not to philosophize a trifle. A great many foolish things have been said there, but one excellent thing has been done. The Republic has been kept along; the silver cord has not been allowed altogether to loose. By hook and by crook, through thick and thin, by something that seemed at times like a clumsy accident, the Republic has been weaned from babyhood and set on its feet. There are plenty of people who promise you it can't walk alone— that it will tumble over and crack its pate. But these are no true friends of the family. The wisest of the doctors and nurses declare that if it is given a chance it will toddle; and now, fortunately, every year its legs are growing longer. In the very place where the monarchs of the last century, as they looked about them at a court that ventured to laugh at honest Molière only when they had given the permissive smile, must have felt peculiarly and transcendently monarchical—beneath that great gilded angel above the proscenium, straddling upon her wrinkled silver cloud and clasping the lilied shield of the Bourbons—under these incongruous circumstances the work has been done. The Assembly has been accused of dragging on its existence longer than was needful for selfish ends, but among these personal joys—that of sitting in the Versailles Theater (I allude to the simple physical act)—cannot be counted. Never were Deputies more uncomfortable. Seven hundred men are packed into a space none too large to accommodate 300; their benches are hardly more ample than the top rail of a fence, and their desks are about the capacity of the book rack in a church pew. As the most significant doings are generally the simplest, there is nothing in what I saw in the Assembly that especially invites narration. Seven hundred gentlemen filed slowly before the tribune and dropped a ballot into an urn. It was a good chance to make a study of the multitudinous types of the French physiognomy, and I endeavored to profit by my opportunity, but one's shorthand notes on such an occasion are rather hard to transcribe.

I just now mentioned M. Taine's new book, which is the literary event of the day, and is very well worth speaking of. The history of the French Revolution, upon which he has so long been engaged, proves to be a work of the somewhat larger scope, which the title I quoted above would indicate. The first volume, a stout

octavo of 550 pages, came out two or three days since;
it is devoted to the "Ancien Régime." M. Taine has
been so much translated that he has now, to English
eyes, a tolerably distinct physiognomy. With the exception of M. Renan, he is now the most brilliant
French writer, albeit that he is not in the Academy.
But in truth, with his extraordinary store of general
knowledge and his magnificent skill in that office, which
is considered the peculiar function of academies—
presentation, exhibition, harmonious arrangement—M.
Taine is an academy in himself. He is very far from
infallible, and so are academies; but like them, right or
wrong, he always speaks with a certain accumulated authority. I speak of him advisedly as a "writer," for
although he is also a logician, a metaphysician, a
thinker, and a scholar, it is the literary quality of his
genius that I most highly relish. I suspect, moreover,
that it is the side that he most relishes himself, and
that, on the whole, it is the most valuable side. Some of
his theories have been severely riddled by criticism, but
at the worst he is capital reading. His style in his present work flows in as ample a current as ever; one sees
that it has been fed from many sources. His theories
here, moreover, are not obtrusive. His work has been
chiefly one of narration and exposition. He has given
a complete picture of the structure and condition of
the French society that preceded the Revolution—its
organization, its habits, its occupations, its public and
private economy, its diet, its costume, its temper, its
ideas, its ways of feeling. The picture is extraordinarily

complete, and is executed with that sustained vigor of which M. Taine only is capable. The eighteenth century in French literature has been turned inside out, sifted and resifted, explored in its minutest detail; but the thing has never been done with the method and energy of M. Taine; there is no other such rich and vivid *résumé*. He has disinterred new facts, possessed himself of new documents, illuminated a variety of points with a stronger light, and made a most interesting book. It is amazing how well we have come to know the eighteenth century; there was never such a labor of revivification. The defunct is standing upon his feet again; he wears his clothes as he used to put them on himself, and his wig as his valet used to powder it; he has the cares of life in his cheeks and the look of sympathy in his eyes; not a wrinkle on his brow, not a detail of his costume is wanting; he can almost speak, or if he cannot speak he easily can listen. If he listens to M. Taine he will hear some painful truths. M. Taine is supposed to intend to take a reactionary view of the French Revolution, and to devote himself chiefly to that somewhat neglected province of history, the injury it did to France. It is high time, certainly, that this work were done, from the liberal and philosophical standpoint. In this volume, however, the author is by no means reactionary; a more damning indictment than his picture of the social orders that the Revolution swept away cannot be imagined. The criticism of what it in turn established will come later. The book is a curious mine of facts about the old royal and aristo-

cratic habits—about the expenditure of the court and
of those who frequented it. I had marked a great many
passages for quotation. Page after page is filled with
accounts of the sinecures under Louis XIV and Louis
XV. Gentlemen and ladies drew ten and twenty thousand francs a year for performing functions which had
not even a name, and others for performing functions which had names which we do not pronounce
in English (they do in French), though the functions
themselves were strictly nominal. The analysis of the
temper and intellectual condition of society is as complete as might have been expected from so keen a psy-
chologist as M. Taine. This is accompanied by a great
many characteristic anecdotes. Louis XIV loved to
centralize; he wished the whole aristocracy to be perpetually at court, paying him its respects. He was
therefore much gratified, I suppose, when a certain
M. de Vardes (the name deserves to be preserved) remarked to him that, "When one is away from your
Majesty, one is not only unhappy; one is ridiculous."
One might be ridiculous, it appears, even within speaking distance of his Majesty. M. Taine speaks of course
of the reign of "sensibility" which set in about the
middle of the last century and continued during the
Revolution, without the least detriment to that of Terror. It produced a great deal of vaporous sentimental-
ity, but it sometimes gave a very delicate point to the
feelings. "We meet thus," says our author, "with ac-
tions and expressions of a supreme grace, unique of
their kind, like some tiny little masterpiece in Sèvres

china." One day when the Countess Amélie de Bouffiers was speaking rather lightly of her husband, her mother-in-law said, "You forget that you are speaking of my son." "It is true," she answered, "I thought I was speaking only of your son-in-law." The virtuous and temperate Madame Élizabeth had sixty thousand dollars allowed her annually for her food. There was doubtless a good deal of reason in Talleyrand's saying that "He who had not lived before 1789 did not know the sweetness of living." There was another point of view, however: the last division of M. Taine's volume, and the most interesting, is on the people. But the whole book is to be read.

H. JAMES, JR.
January 8, 1876

4

PARISIAN SKETCHES

Letter from Henry James, Jr.

MEISSONIER'S "BATTLE OF FRIEDLAND"——PURCHASE OF
THE PICTURE BY MR. A. T. STEWART——MERITS AND DE-
MERITS OF THE WORK——THE HOLIDAYS IN PARIS——PIC-
TURESQUENESS OF THE CITY AT EVENTIDE

[FROM A REGULAR CORRESPONDENT OF THE "TRIBUNE"]

PARIS, Dec. 28.—There has been much notice taken
during the last fortnight of a new picture by Meissonier, which has been on exhibition first at the rooms
of an eminent dealer, and then at the Club des Mir-
litons. Any new work by M. Meissonier [1] is of course
noticeable, but the present one has a special claim to
distinction in the fact that it is the largest picture
that has ever proceeded from the hand of that prince
of miniaturists. Besides, as the future possessors of
it, you should know something about it. The picture has been bought by Mr. A. T. Stewart [2] of
New York for the prodigious sum, as I see it affirmed, of 380,000 francs. The thing is exceedingly
clever, but it strikes me as the dearest piece of goods I
have ever had the honor of contemplating. It has, I be-

lieve, what they call in France its "legend"—that little nebulous body of anecdote which hovers, like the tail of a comet, in the rear of every nine days' wonder. The picture was seen in an embryonic condition by Sir Richard Wallace,[3] and purchased in anticipation for 200,000 francs—one half of which was deposited as a pledge in the hands of the dealer. But time elapsed, and Sir Richard Wallace thought better of his bargain; he took back his offer and his $20,000. Meanwhile the picture was completed, and the price also. It was offered to Mr. Stewart for $60,000. He accepted, but this was not all. The dealer bethought himself that this small parallelogram of canvas would pay a duty of $8,000 at the New York Custom House, and he accordingly annexed this trifle to the bill of sale. Then it appeared that M. Meissonier desired to retain the right to exhibit the picture in the Salon of next year, and that the cost of bringing it back across the seas for this purpose would be a matter of $8,000 more. Why it should cost so much to transport a deal box containing a light canvas from New York to Paris is not immediately apparent. It occupies less space than the most emaciated human being, and it eats nothing. But the fare of the picture was superadded to the amount already mentioned, and the American purchaser laid down without flinching—always according to the "legend"—the round sum of 380,000 francs. The picture represents an immense amount of labor, and of acquired science and skill, and one takes, moreover, an acute satisfaction in seeing America stretch out her long arm and rake in, across the green cloth of the wide Atlantic, the highest prizes of the game of civilization. And yet, in spite of these reflections, M. Meissonier's little picture seemed to me dear, as I have said, at $76,000. It must be added, however, that in dealing with so high a talent as Meissonier's, it is very hard to fix the line of division between the fair value and the factitious value. The ability is so extreme, so consummate, so defiant of analysis, that it carries off with an irresistible assurance any claims it may choose to make. To paint so well as that, you say as you stand and look, must be so difficult, must be impossible—to anyone but Meissonier; and if Meissonier is unique, why should he not command the prices of unique things? If there were only one sewing machine in the world, for instance, who can say what might be the pecuniary conditions annexed to its changing hands? And then I humbly confess that if a certain number of persons have been found to agree that such and such an enormous sum is a proper valuation of a picture, a book, or a song at a concert, it is very hard not to be rather touched with awe and to see a certain golden *reflet* in the performance. Indeed, if you do not see it, the object in question becomes perhaps still more impressive—a something too elevated and exquisite for your dull comprehension. M. Meissonier's picture represents one of those Napoleonic episodes which he has so often treated, and of which he has so completely mastered the costume and the historical expression; he entitles it simply "1807." The work is a yard and a half

long and I suppose about three quarters of a yard high.
It is probable that the painter considers it his greatest
achievement, for he has evidently spent a world of care
and research upon it. The critics in general, apparently, are not of this mind; most of them are of the
opinion that the success, on the whole, is not proportionate to the attempt. The artist, I imagine, has desired not so much to represent a particular battle as to
give a superb pictorial expression of the glory of Napoleon at its climax. It was about in 1807 that it
reached its zenith; then there were no clouds nor
intermissions nor lapses. The battle of Eylau was
fought in 1807, but it took place, if I remember
rightly, in the winter, and the ground, in M. Meissonier's picture, is covered with the deep verdure of
June.[4] At any rate Napoleon stands on a mound in
the middle distance, beyond which, beneath a brilliant, lightly dappled sky, a mighty battle is going
on. Around him are his marshals and his aids, em-
broidered on all their seams, as the phrase is, choking
in their stocks and glittering with their orders. The
Emperor strides his white horse, and sits like a Caesar
on a monument, to return the salute of the troops that
are sweeping past him. M. Meissonier paints him at the
moment when he was probably handsomest, the mid-
season between the meagerness of his earlier years and
the livid corpulence of his later ones. He looks in this
portrait, small as it is, prodigiously like a man to believe in. The foreground of the picture, to the right, is
occupied by a troop of cuirassiers, who are galloping

into action; they are the *morituri* who salute the Caesar
Imperator, and they form the real subject of the work.
They are magnificently painted, and full, I will not say
of movement—Meissonier, to my sense, never represents
it—but of force and completeness of detail. This colo-
nel is exactly passing the spectators, to whom, as he
twists himself in his saddle to lift his saber and bellow
forth his *"Vive l'Empereur!"* he turns his back. His
pose, with its stiffened elongated leg, its contortion in
the saddle, its harmony with the thundering gallop of
the horse, is admirably rendered. Behind him come
plunging and rattling the others, with their long swords
flashing white in the blue air, their heads thrown back
and turned to the Emperor, their mouths wide open,
their acclamations almost audible, their equipments
flapping and jingling, and their horses straining and
clattering in a common impetus. They are trampling
through the high, poppy-strewn grass, where the
crushed flowers seem already like the spatter of blood.
To the left there is a slight interval, filled, in the distance, with the gleam of maneuvering squadrons, beyond which comes riding forward a group of gorgeous
hussars. It bothered the spectators a little that they
should look as if they might come into collision, diag-
onally, with the cuirassiers. They are riding slowly,
however, and they may sit under their great furred bon-
nets and watch the charge. All this goes on in a glare
of sunshine; there are no clouds, no shadows; nothing
but high lights and unrelieved colors. This sustained
unity of light, as it were, is, I take it, a great achieve-

ment, and must have won much applause from people who have attempted similar feats. The picture has extraordinary merits, but I have seen works of a slighter ability that have pleased me more.

It is hard, however, to admire it restrictively without seeming to admire it less than one really does. It seems to me it is a thing of parts rather than an interesting whole. The parts are admirable, and the more you analyze them the better they seem. The best thing, say, is a certain cuirassier, and in the cuirassier the best thing is his clothes, and in his clothes the best thing is his leather straps, and in his leather straps the best thing is the buckles. This is the kind of work you find yourself performing over the picture; you may go on indefinitely. The great general impression which, first and foremost, it is the duty of an excellent picture to give you, seems to me to be wanting here. M. Meissonier is the great archaeologist of the Napoleonic era; he understands to a buttonhole the uniform of the Grand Army. He is equally familiar with the facial types, and he renders marvelously the bronzed and battered physiognomies that scowl from the deep shadow of shakos and helmets. Each man is perfect, but when M. Meissonier has made him—an elaborate, accomplished historical image—he has done his utmost. He feels under no necessity to do anything with him, to place him in any complex relation with anything else, to make any really imaginative uses of him. This suggests to the observer a want of something which he thinks it a great pity a painter of M. Meissonier's powers should not possess—a want intellectual, moral, spiritual; I hardly know what to call it. He resents the attempt to interest him so closely in costume and type, and he privately clamors for an idea. It is this "idea" that is somehow conspicuous by its absence in M. Meissonier's pictures; and yet in so eminent a painter you cannot help looking for it. But, to my sense, they are dry and cold. Look at them beside a Gérôme, indeed, and they seem to bloom and teem with high suggestions; but look at them beside a Delacroix or a Millet and they appear only brilliantly superficial. It is a difference like the difference to the eye between plate glass and gushing water.

But why should I talk of pictures when Paris itself, for the last few days, has formed an immense and brilliant picture. French babies, I believe, hang up their stocking—or put a shoe into the stove—on New Year's Eve; but Christmas, nevertheless, has been very good-humoredly kept. I have never seen Paris so charming as on this last Christmas Day. The weather put in a claim to a share in the fun, the sky was radiant and the air as soft and pure as a southern spring. It was a day to spend in the streets and all the world did so. I passed it strolling half over the city and wherever I turned I found the entertainment that a pedestrian relishes. What people love Paris for became almost absurdly obvious: charm, beguilement, diversion were stamped upon everything. I confess that, privately, I kept thinking of Prince Bismarck and wishing he might take a turn upon the boulevards. Not that they would have flustered him much, I suppose, for, after all, the boulevards are not human; but the whole spectacle seemed a supreme reminder of the fact so constantly present at this time to the reflective mind—the amazing elasticity of France. Beaten and humiliated on a scale without precedent, despoiled, dishonored, bled to death financially—all this but yesterday—Paris is today in outward aspect as radiant, as prosperous, as instinct with her own peculiar genius as if her sky had never known a cloud. The friendly stranger cannot refuse an admiring glance to this mystery of wealth and thrift and energy and good spirits. I don't know how Berlin looked on Christmas Day, though Christmas-keeping is a German specialty, but I greatly doubt whether its aspect would have appealed so irresistibly to the sympathies of the impartial observer. With the approach of Christmas here the whole line of the boulevards is bordered on each side with a row of little booths for the sale—for the sale of everything conceivable. The width of the classic asphalt is so ample that they form no serious obstruction, and the scene, in the evening especially, presents a picturesque combination of the rustic fair and the highest Parisian civilization. You may buy anything in the line of trifles in the world, from a cotton nightcap to an orange neatly pricked in blue letters with the name of the young lady—Adèle or Ernestine—to whom you may gallantly desire to present it. On the other side of the crowded channel the regular shops present their glittering portals, decorated for the occasion with the latest refinements of the trade. The confectioners in particular are amazing; the rows of marvelous *bonbonnières* look like precious sixteenth-century caskets and reliquaries, chiseled by Florentine artists, in the glass cases of great museums. The *bonbonnière*, in its elaborate and impertinent uselessness, is certainly the consummate flower of material luxury; it seems to bloom, with its petals of satin and its pistils of gold, upon the very apex of the tree of civilization.

I walked over to Notre Dame along the quays, and was more than ever struck with the brilliant picturesqueness of Paris as, from any point opposite to the Louvre, you look up and down the Seine. The huge towers of Notre Dame, rising with their blue-gray tone from the midst of the great mass round which the river divides, the great Arc de Triomphe answering them with equal majesty in the opposite distance, the splendid continuous line of the Louvre between, and over it all the charming coloring of Paris on certain days— the brightness, the pearly grays, the flicker of light, the good taste, as it were, of the atmosphere—all this is an entertainment which even custom does not stale. In the midst of it the good people were trudging in thousands, on their various festive errands, well dressed and well disposed. Every tenth man one sees in the streets at present is a soldier, and though this fact has doubtless a melancholy meaning in the moral scale, it has a high value in the picturesque. The cuirassiers especially are numerous, and their glittering helmets light up the crowd. The mass of buildings in front of

Notre Dame has been removed within the last couple
of years, and the open space across which you approach
the church is of immense extent. It is quite the ideal
"chance" for a great cathedral. Notre Dame profits
by it, and her noble façade looks more impressive than
ever. I went in and listened to vespers, and watched the
sounding nave grow dusky and the yellow light turn
pale on the eastern clerestory, and then I wandered
away and crossed the river farther, and climbed that
imperceptible eminence known as the "mountain" of
St. Geneviève, and bent my steps to the curious Church
of St. Étienne du Mont—the church that hides its
florid little Renaissance façade behind the huge neo-
classic drum of the Pantheon. Here I was only in time
for the sermon, but, with all respect to French pulpit
eloquence, which often has a most persuasive grace, it
was time enough. I turned, before long, a deaf ear to
the categories of virtue and vice—it was like the dread-
ful nomenclature of chemistry—and wandered apart
to the shrine of St. Geneviève. The bones of this holy
woman repose in a great brazen tomb in one of the
chapels, surrounded with votive tapers. The scene was
very picturesque. A number of women were on their
knees around it, in the illumined dusk, presenting various objects to be blessed. A young priest opened a sort
of circular lid in the sepulcher, held the object down
into the hole, murmured something over it, and restored it. Some of the articles exposed to the influence
of the beatific ashes were singularly prosaic. One, for
instance, was a clean shirt, rigidly plaited and starched.

The motive of this application puzzled me; was the applicant a laundress? She was probably the pious relative of a sick man who was contemplating a change of linen. In either case, I seemed to have walked far away from the boulevards, and from the Christmas Day of 1875.

HENRY JAMES, JR.

January 22, 1876

5

THE PARISIAN STAGE

Letter from Henry James, Jr.

THE DRAMA AS IT IS——POPULARITY OF "OPÉRA BOUFFE"
——ROSSI AS MACBETH——SUCCESS OF SARDOU'S "FERRÉOL"
——DEARTH OF NEW PIECES

[FROM A REGULAR CORRESPONDENT OF THE "TRIBUNE"]

PARIS, Jan. 7.—That the theater plays in Paris a
larger part in people's lives than it does anywhere else
is by this time a fact too well established to need especial comment. It is one of the first facts that comes
under the observation of the resident foreigner, who
very soon perceives that the theater is an essential part
of French civilization, in regard to which it keeps up
a lively process of action and reaction. It is not a mere
amusement, as it is in other countries; it is an interest,
an institution, connected through a dozen open doors
with literature, art, and society. There are, of course,
plenty of people who assure you that the French stage
of today is nothing but a name; that its great days are
over, and that to know the perfection of acting one
should have been born seventy years ago. Born, unfortunately, more recently, I have seen neither Talma, nor

Mlle. Mars, nor Mlle. Georges, nor Madame Dorval, nor Rachel, nor Frédéric Lemaître, and in such a case, though it is disagreeable to have to assent to invidious reflections, it is difficult to gainsay them.[1] But even without this questionable privilege of depressing comparison, I must add that I find it easy to imagine the French stage being better than it is. I remember vaguely Rose Chéri, and distinctly Mlle. Desclée.[2] The best acting in Paris is extremely good, at the present time, but the second best is not so much better than it is elsewhere, as it is sometimes assumed to be. I take it that the sign of a highly flourishing state of dramatic art is excellence in secondary positions—finish in out-of-the-way places. This is what Mr. Ruskin praises in the art of the greatest architecture, and the analogy may be carried into the labors of the actor. Is it true, then, that the golden days of the French stage are over? I shall not pretend to say, but I think that a critic of greater courage might find some support for an affirmative answer. He might, indeed, while he was about it, go on to argue that the happy time of the acted drama has passed away the world over. He might, if he were philosophically inclined, remark that the dramatic art requires, both in performers and spectators, a certain simplicity, a naïveté, an abeyance of the critical spirit which are rapidly passing out of human life. To produce very good acting there should be a class of performers and a public in whom subtlety has not attained its maximum. If evidence in favor of this assertion were needed, I should venture to point to

two striking cases of essentially modern acting which
I have lately witnessed as samples of the harm that can
be done by the absence of what I have called naïveté.
One is the Macbeth of Mr. Henry Irving, which I lately
saw in London; the other is the Macbeth of Signor
Ernesto Rossi, which I saw the other night here. I do
not know how Garrick or Charles Kemble or Edmund
Kean [3] played the part, or how Talma would have
played it if he had been allowed: but as I watched the
English and the Italian tragedian I murmured within
myself, "Oh, for one touch of Kemble or of Talma!"
one touch of good faith, of the ideal, the simple. But
Irving and Rossi are very clever actors, and these remarks have perhaps an air of aberration. So far as
such matters in Paris are concerned, it may be enough
to allude, in confirmation of a gloomy view of the future of the stage, to the inordinate prosperity, of late
years, of *opéra bouffe*. This phenomenon, I should say,
could only have been possible in a community which
had ceased to take the theater with that degree of seriousness which is necessary for its perfect good health.

A person fond of the stage and indifferent to *opéra
bouffe* has not just now a very comfortable time of it.
At least a third of the theaters are given over to the
strains of Offenbach, of Lecocq, and of Hervé,[4] and the
photographs of the actresses who impart to these melo-
dies the requisite complement of grimace and gesture,
simper at you from every second shopwindow. My
present complaint of the *Cruche Cassée* and the *Créole* [5]
is not that they are vulgar or trivial or indecent, but

simply that they are unhistrionic. They give up the
stage to something which not only is not acting, but
is a positive denial of acting. To act is to produce an
illusion; to interpret Offenbach is to snap your fingers
and thrust out your tongue at illusion—to try and
make it appear that a young woman in the audience,
too frolicsome, really, to be suffered to go at large, has
scrambled upon the stage and is using the footlights
in the interest of her sentimental relations with a plu-
rality of individuals in the house. The favorite actress
in *opéra bouffe* at the present hour is Mme. Judic,[6] an
extremely pretty woman. An inventory of Mme. Judic's
artistic stock in trade would be really a very curious
document. After Mme. Judic in popular favor comes
Céline Chaumont, who is not nearly so pretty, but in-
finitely cleverer. Mme. Chaumont is indeed so clever,
and has such genuine dramatic gifts, that it is very
dismal to see what *opéra bouffe* is making of her.

The winter season is in full operation at the theaters,
but I hardly know upon what novelties to confer the
honor of an especial mention. I have already spoken
of Rossi, to whom I just now alluded. He pursues his
triumphant career, and having exhausted the popularity of Kean, has added Macbeth to his Shakespearean
performances.[7] His acting in this part, as in every
other, is at once very fine and very coarse. I should say
he was poorest in the best places and best in the com-
paratively unimportant ones. In this he resembles Mr.
Henry Irving, who is so meager in the essential and
so redundant in the (relatively) superfluous. Rossi is

a superb stage figure, and every now and then he has
a cry, a movement, a look, which goes straight to the
mark; but, as a whole, I thought his Macbeth a decidedly bungling affair. It was ludicrously Italian—
I am sorry to associate so disrespectful an adverb with
so glorious an adjective. It is true, however, that in
most cases of an alternation of good taste and bad, the
genius of modern Italy decides for the bad. The scene
of Duncan's murder is disfigured by the most absurd
ventriloquial effects on the part of the shuddering
Thane, who makes an elaborate attempt to give his
wife an idea of the way the voices of the sleeping
grooms sounded. Fancy the distracted chieftain reeling
out red-handed from his crime and beginning to give
"imitations." The scene with Banquo's ghost was disappointing, and the address to the specter singularly
weak. It is a good indication of Rossi's caliber that he
depends for his final effect here upon a very puerile
piece of ingenuity. The scene has been vulgarly acted
and vulgarly declaimed; Signor Rossi has been reserv-
ing himself. And for what? As Macbeth leaves the
apartment with his wife, after the departure of the
guests, he stumbles upon his long mantle, trips, falls,
and rolls over with his heels in the air. His mind is so
full of supernatural horrors that he thinks the ghost
of Banquo is still playing him tricks, and he lies crouch-
ing and quaking, to see what is coming next. It is a
handsome somersault, certainly, but I do not think it
can be called acting Shakespeare. The actress who
plays Lady Macbeth with Signor Rossi has obtained

a great success—a success which owes nothing to felicity of costume. I spoke just now of "good faith," and of Italian bad taste; Mme. Pareti-Glech puts these two things together and produces a striking result. The Italians, after all, if you make them a certain allowance, have an instinctive sense of the picturesque which is beyond our culture. Grant that Lady Macbeth's influence over her husband was a purely physical one, and this obscure southern artist is superb. You should see the gesture with which, in her call upon nature to "unsex" herself, she utters the great "Hold, hold!"—or those with which, to raise Macbeth to his senses before the visitors who have been knocking at the gate are admitted, she shakes him about and chokes him by his coat collar.

The most successful play of the winter, up to this time, has been the *Ferréol* of Victorien Sardou, and it is an agreeable fact that it is also the best. It is consummately clever, in M. Sardou's usual way, and is acted at the Gymnase in a manner to throw its cleverness into extraordinary relief. It literally palpitates with interest, as the phrase is, and from the first word and to the last the spectator is under the charm. The charm with M. Sardou is not of a very high quality; he makes a play very much as he would make a pudding; he has his well-tested recipe and his little stores of sugar and spice, from which he extracts with an unimpassioned hand exactly the proper quantity of each. The pudding is capital, but I can think of no writer of equal talent who puts so little of himself into his writing. Search M. Sardou's plays through and you will not find a trace of a personal conviction, of a moral emotion, of an intellectual temperament, of anything that makes the "atmosphere" of a work. They seem to have been produced in a sort of mental vacuum. But they are not played in a vacuum by any means, and *Ferréol* bids fair to run for a good part of the rest of the winter. It has made the reputation, and, theatrically, the fortune of an admirable young actor named Worms.[8] I don't know when I have seen a piece of acting that has given me such unmitigated satisfaction as M. Worms's representation of the distracted hero of this piece. He has seen a man murdered as he himself was leaving clandestinely at two o'clock in the morning the house of the woman he loves, and his lips are sealed by the fact of his position. His best friend is arrested on suspicion and condemned by the strongest circumstantial evidence, and yet he cannot make a declaration which involves publication of the circumstance that his point of view, as a witness, was the garden wall of Mme. de Bois-Martel. This lady (who had imprudently permitted his visit) is in equal distress, and the unhappy couple are buffeted to and fro between the sense of their duty and of their dangers. I need not say how the problem is solved, for sooner or later, I suppose, *Ferréol* will be "adapted." But in losing M. Worms it will lose half its power. This young actor has a gift of quiet realism, of mingled vehemence and discretion, of impassioned self-control, which places him at a jump beside Delaunay,[9] the classic *jeune premier* of the Théâtre

Français, whom, however, he resembles only in the perfection of his art. The Français has promptly marked him for her own. Under her fostering care he can ripen and develop at his ease.

Actors are just now indeed rather too much at their ease at this establishment, which has produced this winter but a single new piece—a little one-act comedy by M. Pailleron.[10] When the Théâtre Français can do nothing else, as a critic said the other day, she can drape herself in her majesty—she can draw from her immense historical repertory. The drapery is most voluminous and becoming, but the terms of the Théâtre Français's magnificent contract with the state are that she shall increase her inheritance and think of the future as well as the past. M. Pailleron's comedy, *Petite Pluie* by name, has had a moderate success, which it owes wholly to the incomparable skill of Mme. Plessy.[11] There is a double interest in watching Mme. Plessy, as with the present winter she is to close her long and brilliant career. She has probably never done anything more purely brilliant than the part she plays in the piece I have just mentioned. The comedy treats of a young woman who has eloped from a villa on the French Riviera, near the Italian frontier, with a secretary of legation, and who arrives with her lover in her ball dress at a wayside inn, to which the guilty couple have been driven by a sudden storm and by a fracture of the shafts of their carriage. Here they are overtaken by the friend from whose domicile, while paying her a visit and dancing at her ball, the fair fugitive has fled

—a clever woman of the world, who disapproves altogether of elopements, takes a skeptical view of love, and
recommends Mme. de Thiais to return to her husband,
shabby fellow as he is. While the secretary of legation
is out under the shed, pottering over his broken shaft
with the drowsy innkeeper, the two ladies have it out
together. The elder one riddles her friend's illusions
with her wit, gives her a wholesome fright, and with a
curtsy to the naughty attaché takes her off under her
arm. This scene is acted by Mme. Plessy with a spirit
and style and grace—what the French call an authority—which are certainly the last word of high comedy.
Mme. Plessy is not (to my thinking) a woman of
genius; she is not even a sympathetic actress; there is
something always rather hard and metallic in her style.
But she is so consummate, so accomplished, so perfect
a mistress of the subtlest resources of her art, that to
follow her through the light and shade of a long speech
is not merely an amusement, but a real intellectual
profit. When I think of all the experience, the observation, the reflection, the contact with life and art which
are summed up in such a mellow maturity of skill, I am
struck with a kind of veneration. Of the other theaters
there is nothing very important to narrate. The *Revue*
prevails at several of them, notably at the Variétés,[12]
which is supposed to be its stronghold—that dreary,
flimsy burlesque of the events of the year, which is
the pretext for so many bad jokes and undressed *fi-
gurantes*. The Palais Royal is, as always, exhaustingly
exhilarating, with *Le Panache*,[13] a long farce in which

the element of quiet comedy is thought to be more marked than usual. This speaks well for the farces of the past. Lastly, the Vaudeville with *Les Scandales d'Hier*,[14] and a company augmented by Pierre Berton from the Français, and Mlle. Pierson of the Gymnase —mysterious fugitives both—has been expending some very good acting on a very indifferent play.

HENRY JAMES, JR.
January 29, 1876

6

PARISIAN LIFE

Letter from Henry James, Jr.

POLITICS AND THE DRAMA—THE PROGRESS OF THE ELEC-
TORAL CAMPAIGN—MINISTER BUFFET'S DREAD OF "SO-
CIAL PERIL"—THE NEW RUSSIAN DRAMA—THE ACTOR
ROSSI AS ROMEO

[FROM A REGULAR CORRESPONDENT OF THE "TRIBUNE"]

PARIS, Jan. 18.—It seems just now, in writing from
Paris, rather light-minded to speak of anything else
than the political situation, but if one has a decent pretext for holding one's tongue about French politics, I
think one is a great fool not to take advantage of it.
Nothing else, it is true, is talked about.[1] The elections
are all-pervasive, and no one has attention for anything
but the crimes, or the virtues (as he may happen to
consider them), of M. Buffet.[2] There is, of course, an
infinite amount of more or less ferocious discussion, and
every man suspects a political adversary in every other.
When I say that it is a blessing not to be obliged to
discuss, I mean that if one is disposed that way, one
may find at every turn the most vivid reminder of the
vanity of passionate argument. The intensity of politi-

cal discussions is sharper in France than it is anywhere
else—which is the case, indeed, with every sort of difference of opinion. There are more camps and coteries
and "sets" than among Anglo-Saxons, and the gulf
which divides each group from every other is more
hopelessly and fatally impassable.[3] Nothing is more
striking to a foreigner, even after he thinks he has
grown used to such things, than the definiteness with
which people here are classed and ticketed. The ticket
reads so or so, of course, according to your point of
view; but to the man who wears another ticket it always
reads villainously. You ask a writer whose productions
you admire some questions about any other writer, for
whose works you have also a relish. "Oh, he is of the
School of This or That; he is of the *queue* of So and
So," he answers. "We think nothing of him: you
mustn't talk of him here; for us he doesn't exist." And
you turn away, meditative, and perhaps with a little
private elation at being yourself an unconsolidated
American and able to enjoy both Mr. A. and Mr. X.[4]
who enjoy each other so little. Of course subsequently
you do them justice in their mutual aversions, and perceive that some of the qualities you admire in their
writings are really owing to their being intrenched behind their passwords. A little school that dislikes every
other school, but is extremely active and industrious
within its own circle, is an excellent engine for the production of limited perfection, and French literature
abounds in books in which particular tendencies have
been pushed to lengths which only a sort of artistic

conspiracy of many minds could have reached, but which seem like mere blind alleys of thought, where explorers perish, suffocated for want of having taken heed of possible issues to right or left. It is simply the old story that, either in politics or in literature, Frenchmen are ignorant of the precious art of compromise. The imagination sinks helpless before the idea of a Monarchist and a Republican ever really coming to terms. The Legitimists the other day formed a temporary coalition with the Republicans for the sake of keeping the Orleanists out of the Senate, but this was not because they loved the Republicans more, but because they loved the Orleanists less. And yet this sounds almost like blasphemy in presence of the fact that the Republic is every day making converts from the monarchical ranks.

Nothing succeeds like success, and it must seem to any sensible Frenchman, who is not a simple partisan, that the excellent position of France before the world at the present time offers really no decent pretext for pretending that the Republic is not sufficient and safe. But it is nevertheless true that every convert the present regime makes is a supreme testimony to the force of good example and of liberal ideas. This is the more true that a deplorable example is being so continually offered to recalcitrant patriots by M. Buffet—the agitated minister of a profoundly tranquil country, as *Le Temps*, a day or two ago, very happily called him. To an unattached outsider like myself, who has nothing but his personal impressions to go by, M. Buffet seems bent on goading a thoroughly well-disposed and well-conducted country to desperation. His theory is that however well-conducted France may be, she is so only by compulsion and so long as she feels the strong hand, and that she is not in the least well disposed. All his talk is of "social peril," but no one can in the least imagine what he means. To keep the country quiet he sticks needles into her, and to set an example of mutual confidence he shakes his watchman's rattle. M. Buffet is a frightened man; he has never recovered from the Commune.[5] The Commune was certainly not reassuring, but it weighs lightly in the scale compared with the general attitude of the country, which considers that the Republic has established fair ground for presumption in its favor, which has a desire for rest and peace and work and order at least as lively as the Prime Minister's, and which believes that the best guarantee of these comforts is a frank acceptance of the Republic. It is probable that this will be sufficiently manifested in the result of the general elections, which began yesterday by the election of delegates by the municipal councils. The rural districts are with the present occasion to express themselves more directly in political affairs than they have ever done before. Marshal MacMahon [6] has ushered in the campaign with a proclamation which is placarded in all the streets, and which, though it expresses very correct sentiments, strikes me as a rather regrettable performance. A proclamation of the Chief of the State addressed directly to the nation over the heads of the ministry is a step so irregular and abnormal that it should be resorted to only in moments of extraordinary public peril. This is far from being such a moment, and it is paying no compliment to the country at large to assume it to be, and to pretend that the nation is in need of this portentous reminder of the rudimentary duties of patriotism. This is all the proclamation contains, with the exception of a more satisfactory passage, which M. Buffet probably did not enjoy having to countersign, promising that the Marshal will favor no revision of the present Constitution until it has been fairly and loyally tested—which it has not been yet. The proclamation is unfortunate because it interrupts that most desirable process, the formation in France of a tradition in favor of impersonal government. Such a tradition is slowly and laboriously shaping itself, and every month that France continues both prosperous and parliamentary will lend it more authority. But I think it can be said that the document in question has neither unduly discomposed nor unduly comforted the mass of good citizens.

I went too far just now in saying that nothing but politics is talked about: everyone finds a word for *Les Danicheff* [7] and I suppose that I should therefore find a word for them too. *Les Danicheff* is a drama of mysterious origin which has just been brought out with extraordinary success at the Odéon Theater, and is attracting all Paris to that remote and unfriended establishment. Its origin is as mysterious as anything can be with which M. Alexandre Dumas is associated—for

the play has been largely retouched and manipulated
by him. It is the work of a Russian author who calls
himself on the bills, fictitiously, M. Pierre Newsky, but
who is otherwise unknown. The story goes that he
brought his drama a year ago to the author of the
Demi-Monde to ask his opinion of it, and that Dumas
replied that the subject was magnificent but the treatment in a high degree clumsy. Then, by way of pointing out errors, he sat down with his docile petitioner
and fairly made the play over. Its success is in a great
measure owing to the more famous author's remarkable
scenic science which forms a distinct and easily recog-
nizable ingredient. The smartness is all Dumas'—the
epigrams, the tirades, the aphorisms, by this time
rather drearily familiar, about the fathomless depravity of the female sex. But the theme of the piece is so
picturesque and effective that it carries Dumas' faults
hardly less easily than his merits. It has the charm of
being strange and novel, and not dealing with the ever-
lasting seventh commandment as interpreted on the
boulevards. In spite of this, however, the story is easier
to tell in French than in English. A Russian countess
of autocratic temper picks out a wife for her only son,
the ardent and gallant young Vladimir. He declines his
mother's offer, and intimates that he is in love with a
young girl, by birth a serf, whom she has educated and
admitted into her drawing room. Scandalized and hor-
rified, she attempts to reason away his passion, but he
is deaf to arguments and threats, and insists upon
marrying the modest and amiable Anna. The Countess

obtains of him that he will at least absent himself for a
year from home, to test the permanency of his affection
—that he will repair to Moscow, frequent the society of
his equals, and do his best to fall in love. He departs,
and as soon as his back is turned she summons Anna
and marries her, willy-nilly, out of hand, to the coachman. The coachman, a certain Osip, in his black velvet
knickerbockers and his red silk caftan, is the real hero
of the piece. The scene of the marriage is very effective,
and makes a striking picture—all the serfs convoked
and ranged solemnly round, the long-bearded pope,
the picturesque moujik, with a soul above his station,
the high-handed old Countess in the middle, flanked by
her parrot, her lap dog, and her two grotesque and
servile old lady companions, and the poor young girl,
vainly entreating and sobbing, in the pitying silence,
and twisting herself at the feet of her mistress. Her resistance and her prayers are vain, and, secretly in love
as she is with Vladimir, she is shuffled into the arms of
Osip. The coachman is an old-time comrade of the heir
of the house, who, when they were boys together, had
treated him almost as an equal, and toward whom he
has always preserved a devoted loyalty. Vladimir, on
hearing of Anna's marriage, comes back from Moscow
like a whirlwind, long before his year is out, and his
savage irruption, whip in hand, into the cottage of the
humble couple produces a great effect. This is so well
rendered by the young actor who plays the part that
the audience breaks out into long applause before he
has spoken a word. Then follows a scene between the

two young men which it required some delicacy to handle. The upshot of it is that Osip, instead of deserving his young master's opprobrium for what he has done, has earned his gratitude. He has contented himself with being Anna's husband but in name—he has piously abstained from the exercise of marital rights— he has accepted the young girl (whom, of course, he secretly adores), only as a sacred deposit. The marriage shall be broken and he will hand her over to Vladimir. I need nol relate the conclusion of the piece, for after this exalted flight the most felicitous conclusion must be more or less of an anticlimax. The obvious objection to the story is that Osip is too ethereal a fellow for a Russian coachman: but the authors have made him plausible, the part is singularly well played, and for myself, I do not object to fanciful creation. What I enjoyed in *Les Danicheff*, in spite of the very sensible presence of Dumas, is a certain imaginative good faith and naïveté which offer a grateful change from the familiar gyrations of that terribly tough and lean old performer, *l'esprit parisien*.

I have it on my conscience, while touching on these matters, to say another word about Ernesto Rossi, of whom I have spoken hitherto with a certain meagerness of praise. He has lately appeared as Romeo,[8] and though he has attracted less attention in the part than in some others, it is the one in which he has given me most pleasure. He has scandalously mutilated the play, but there is a certain compensation in the fact that what he has left of it sounds wonderfully well in Italian. One

never sees Shakespeare played without being reminded
at some new point of his greatness: the other night what
struck me was the success with which, for the occasion,
he had Italianized his fancy. The things that trouble
us nowadays in *Romeo and Juliet*—the redundancy of
protestation, the importunate conceits, the embarras-
sing frankness—all these fall into their place in the
rolling Italian diction, and what one seems to see is not
a translation, but a restitution. It is singular that Rossi
should play best the part that he looks least, for a
stout, middle-aged man one would say that Romeo was
rather a snare. But it is with Romeo very much as with
Juliet; by the time an actor has acquired the assurance
necessary for playing the part, he has lost his youth
and his slimness. Robust and mature as he is, Rossi
does it as a consummate artist; it is impossible to imagine anything more picturesquely tender, more intensely
ardent. As I have said, he has done very much what
he chose with the play, but it is not to be denied that
in one or two cases he has almost made his modifica-
tions pardonable. He makes Juliet come to her senses
in the tomb and discover her inanimate lover before
Romeo has utterly expired. Besides enabling the hap-
less couple to perish in each other's arms, this gives
Rossi an opportunity for a great stroke of dumb show
—the sort of thing in which he decidedly excels. He has
staggered away from the tomb while the poison, which
he has just drunk, is working, and stands with his back
to it as Juliet noiselessly revives and emerges. He returns to it, finds it empty, looks about him, and sees

Juliet standing a short distance off, and looking in the dim vault like a specter. He has been bending over the empty tomb, and his eyes fall upon her as he slowly rises. His movement of solemn terror as he slowly throws up his arms and continues to rise and rise, until, with his whole being dilated, he stands staring and appalled, on tiptoe, is, although it is grotesque in description, very well worth seeing. Rossi's speeches are often weak, but when he attempts an acutely studied piece of pantomime he never misses it. This superiority of his pantomime to his delivery seems to me to fix him, in spite of his great talent, in the second line of actors.

HENRY JAMES, JR.
February 5, 1876

7

PARISIAN TOPICS

Letter from Henry James, Jr.

VICTOR HUGO'S ADDRESS TO THE COMMUNAL DELEGATES
—FRENCH NATIONAL VANITY—THE LAMARTINE MONU-
MENT—PARISIAN "CONFÉRENCES"—THE PAINTER PILS'S
CAREER AND WORKS

[FROM A REGULAR CORRESPONDENT OF THE "TRIBUNE"]

PARIS, Jan. 28.—The newspapers for the last fortnight have contained little else than addresses and pro-
grams from candidates for the Senate and the Cham-
bers. One of the most remarkable documents of this
kind is a sort of *pronunciamiento* from Victor Hugo,[1]
who is not indeed a possible Senator or Deputy, but
who has been nominated delegate to the electoral college of the Seine for the election of Senators. The election in this department promises to wear a rather
ruddy hue, and if M. Hugo's utterances have any influence upon it, it will certainly be red enough. We shall
see, however, for it comes off on the thirtieth of the
month. It seems incredible that Victor Hugo's political
vaticinations should have a particle of influence upon
any human creature; but I have no doubt that they re-

verberate sonorously enough in some of the obscurer
couches sociales, and there is no reason indeed why the
same influences which shaped Victor Hugo should not
have produced a number of other people who are like
him in everything except in having genius. But in these
matters his genius does not count, for it is certainly
absent enough from his address to the "delegates of the
36,000 communes of France." It might have been believed that he had already given the measure of the
power of the human mind to delude itself with mere
words and phrases, but his originality in this direction
is quite unequaled, and perhaps I did wrong to say
that there was no genius in it. There is, at any rate, a
genius for pure verbosity. What he has to say to his
36,000 brother delegates is that "Babylon has the hero-
ism of Saragossa," that "upon this Paris which merited
all venerations have been heaped all affronts," that the
world "has measured the quantity of insult it has
poured forth to the quantity of respect that was owed."
It is worth quoting. "What matters, however? In taking from her her diadem as capital of France, her enemies have laid bare her brain as capital of the world.
This great forehead of Paris is now entirely visible, all
the more radiant that it is discrowned. Henceforth the
nations unanimously recognize Paris as the leading
city of the human race." M. Hugo proceeds to summon
his electors "to decree the end of abuses by the advent
of truths, to affirm France before Germanism, Paris before Rome, light before night." Whether or not as a
nation the French are more conceited than their neigh-

bors is a question that may be left undecided; a very
good case on this charge might be made out against
every nation. But certainly France occasionally produces individuals who express the national conceit with
a transcendent fatuity which is not elsewhere to be
matched. A foreign resident in the country may speak
upon this point with feeling; it makes him extremely
uncomfortable. I don't know how it affects people who
dislike French things to see their fantastic claims for
their spiritual mission in the world, but it is extremely
disagreeable for those who like them. Such persons desire to enjoy in a tranquil and rational manner the
various succulent fruits of French civilization, but they
have no fancy for being committed to perpetual genu-
flections and prostrations. They read Victor Hugo's
windy sublimities in the evening paper over their profanely well-cooked dinners, and probably on leaving
the restaurant their course lies along the brilliantly illuminated boulevard. The aspect of the boulevards, of
a fine, mild evening, is as cheerful as you please, but it
exhibits a number of features which are not especially
provocative of "veneration." Perhaps the irritated foreigner we are imagining is going to hear the *Timbale
d'Argent* or the *Petite Mariée* [2] and he asks himself at
what particular point of these compositions the brain
of the capital of the world is laid bare. A good
many other things are laid bare, but brain is not
among them. Of course Victor Hugo, as a political
adviser, is taken *au sérieux* by very few people, but
the fact remains that one is liable to meet him in this

character in one's evening paper; and it is an amusing fact.

Victor Hugo's old poetic rival, or rather his brother in the Muse, the generous Castor of this impetuous Pollux, has also just been having an hour's reappearance as an "actuality." A very brilliant performance was given the other day at the Porte Saint-Martin Theater in aid of the fund for erecting a statue to Alphonse de Lamartine.[3] This is always found to be the most effective way of raising money in France, and it generally produces large sums. People who will not put down their names for a franc on a subscription paper will joyously pay the requisite fee for the privilege of jamming themselves into an ill-placed seat in a crowded theater on that least inspiring of occasions, a morning performance. The other day the program was attractive, as several of Lamartine's most famous poems were declaimed and sung by artists of the Théâtre Français and the Opera. It is worth a little discomfort to hear some fine verses recited by Delaunay and Mlle. Favart.[4] There is no better proof, however, that the good Homer sometimes nods, than that that somewhat lurid star of the same establishment—the young tragedian, M. Mounet-Sully [5]—should be allowed in the matter of recitation to (in vulgar parlance) "go on" as he does. He is a clever actor, but he has no conception of the proper way to treat beautiful lyric verse— to let it speak for itself. His rantings and sputterings and contortions are altogether beside the mark, and it is hard to understand how, in so august a school, he

should have been permitted to form such habits. I believe he is a very willful young man. The *pièce de ré-
sistance* on the occasion I mention was a *conférence* by
M. Ernest Legouvé,[6] the prince of *conférenciers*. This
epithet may be interpreted as a compliment in any degree the reader chooses. A *conférence* (the reader may
need to be reminded) is a performance which generally
takes place in a very uncomfortable little room on the
Boulevard des Capucines, into which curiosity has occasionally beguiled my steps. It is both something more
than a lecture, in our sense of the word, and something
less—more by grace, but decidedly less by exertion.
The French talk offhand so much more neatly and brilliantly than we who have to buffet the big billows of
the English tongue can ever hope to do that almost
any clever man who will mount beside a desk with a
glass of water beside him is a very sufficient lecturer.
Perhaps that is the reason why the spectacle of such
a personage is so far from attracting a crowd. I have
never been into the room in the Boulevard des Capucines without finding a motive for odd reflections. An
American is brought up to the idea that a lecturer is a
very highly developed personage, and that the profession he exercises is one of the most eminent and lucrative in the world. He has been thankful for standing
room at the Cooper Institute or the Boston Music
Hall,[7] and he has it well in mind that, compared with
Paris, Boston and New York are generally admitted,
in the matter of evening amusements, to be steeped in
barbarism. He is surprised, therefore, to find that the

only hospitality offered here to this ennobling pastime is dispensed in a little dusky, crooked room resembling the cellar of a warehouse or a vacated stable, and that he sometimes comes very near being the sole auditor. Is this the glittering capital of pleasure? he asks; for all the appointments are of the most primitive description. I must frankly confess, however, that they are generally good enough for the *conférence*, which is apt to be of a very slender texture. An American lecture is sometimes "thin" enough, but a *conférence* has an even further degree of transparency. The only gentleman in whose honor I have ever seen the little room in the Boulevard des Capucines filled is M. Francisque Sarcey,[8] the dramatic critic of the *Temps*, and one of the *maîtres du genre*. M. Sarcey may have begun to prepare his lecture ten minutes before his arrival, but I doubt whether it has taken more of his time. It is generally upon some book which has lately appeared, and it is often very entertaining. There could hardly be a better example of the value of practice and of assurance. If M. Sarcey can once begin he is safe. He rubs his hands, drinks a great many glasses of water, gets under way, drifts from one thing to another, and talks out his hour. But at the end of it, though I may have sat reflecting on the mysterious alchemy of the French tongue, agreeably spoken, I have, in retrospect, felt just a trifle bamboozled. It is, of course, very true that I have not been forced to go there, and it is also to be remembered that the sum taken in at the door is of the slenderest. As the maidservant said, when, on her having saved up thirty crowns, she was asked why she married a hunchback, "What sort of a husband can one get for thirty crowns?" [9]

The practice of collecting an artist's works into an exhibition after his death is apparently passing from the exception into the rule. I think it may be said that it is only a rather broad rule that would include the productions of poor M. Pils,[10] who died last autumn, and whose pictures have lately been gathered into the great hall of the École des Beaux Arts, the scene of the exhibition of the works of Barye, which I mentioned the other day. Pils was a military painter of the school, generally speaking, of Horace Vernet [11]—some of whose merits he lacked, however, as well as many of his defects. He was neither so good as Vernet at his best, nor so bad as Vernet when Vernet was worse than usual. His posthumous exhibition, nevertheless, is interesting, and the custom, though it is liable to abuse, seems excellent. It gives an artist another chance, as it were, another bid for fame, after nature has brought down the hammer. Pils's life is more interesting perhaps than his work, and it has been very sympathetically related by M. Becq de Fouquières. He was an immitigable invalid, from the cradle, and his career was a constant battle with disease. He painted the Crimean and the Italian campaigns without being able to follow the army, though he spent some time in Algeria preparing an immense picture of the reception of the native chiefs by the Emperor and Empress. This work, unfortunately, was a rather melancholy failure and is

not exhibited; the Empress, who, I believe, was usually
very obliging in such matters, never succeeded in finding an hour to sit for her portrait, though Pils followed
the court about for weeks, palette in hand, awaiting
his chance. It must be said, in justice, that his women
are not very lovely creations. His specialty was the
French soldier of the Second Empire, the victor of the
Alma and of Magenta, and him he thoroughly understood. His great success was a huge representation of
the battle of the Alma, which now covers one whole side
of the hall of the École des Beaux Arts. Much of this
gigantic canvas is common and empty, but the soldiers
are real soldiers—the zouaves and chasseurs really
move, with all the infinite variety of attitude of the
soldier in action. The idea with Pils, the first sketch,
and the start, were always excellent; he broke down in
the later stages—in consequence, often, of the want of
physical strength. His patience and courage under reiterated interruptions of this kind seem to have been
inexhaustible, and he appears to have had a large
measure of that almost touching simplicity of nature
which is frequent among French artists—as in Millet
and Flandrin.[12] He painted the dome of the staircase
in the new Opera, and the brush dropped from his hand
just as he finished his work. He did not live to suffer
from the silence of the critics about it. Apollo and the
Muses were not in his line, and his pictures were over-
shadowed by the brilliant and exquisite compositions
of M. Baudry in a neighboring part of the building.
But Pils played his part—he erected a monument to

the old military glory of France. It was not his fault if
his pictures had an imponderable influence in precipi-
tating the country into the miseries of 1870. I must add
a word about a greater name than that of Pils.

Two very interesting pictures of Eugène Delacroix [13]
have for some time been visible at Durand-Ruel's. One
is an immense affair, painted in his early youth—a
Sardanapalus upon his funeral pile: it takes early
youth to attack such subjects as that. The luxurious
monarch is reclining upon his cushions on the summit
of a sort of brazen monument, and his jewels and treasures and disheveled wives are heaped in confusion about
him. The subject was not easy, and Delacroix has not
solved its difficulties; much of the picture is very bad,
even for a neophyte. But here and there a passage is
almost masterly, and the whole picture indicates the
dawning of a great imagination. One of the women, half
naked and tumbling over helpless on her face against
the couch of her lord, with her hands bound behind
her, and her golden hair shaken out with her lamenta-
tions, seems, in her young transparent rosiness, like the
work of a more delicate and more spiritual Rubens.
The other picture, painted in 1848, an "Entombment
of Christ," is one of the author's masterpieces, and is
a work of really inexpressible beauty; Delacroix is
there at his best, with his singular profundity of imagination and his extraordinary harmony of color. It is
the only modern religious picture I have seen that
seemed to me painted in good faith, and I wish that
since such things are being done on such a scale it

might be bought in America. It is very dear, but it is to be had, considering what it is, for nothing, compared with Meissonier's "1807."

HENRY JAMES, JR.
February 19, 1876

8

PARIS IN ELECTION TIME

Letter from Henry James, Jr.

THE NEW SENATE——M. GAMBETTA AND CLERICAL EDU-
CATION——EX-MINISTER BUFFET'S PERSONAL OUTLINES——
M. DE GIRARDIN ON THE DUTY OF FRANCE——BONAPARTIST
FANCIES——THE LATE FRÉDÉRIC LEMAÎTRE

[FROM A REGULAR CORRESPONDENT OF THE "TRIBUNE"]

PARIS, Feb. 11.——There is just at present a lull in
the political storm. The elections for the Senate came
off on the thirtieth of last month, and those for the Assembly occur on the twentieth of the present one. You
yourselves learn the facts in these cases a few hours
later. They were such, in the senatorial elections, as to
gratify people who feel at liberty to take, on the whole,
a cheerful view of republican institutions. There were
more Moderate Republicans elected, fewer Radicals,
and very much fewer Bonapartists, than had been
feared. The great news of the day, indeed, was the defeat of the Bonapartists, who muster, at the largest estimate, but forty Senators. The election in Paris was
of a paler hue than had seemed likely. Victor Hugo
was successful, but only on a second ballot, and Louis

Blanc [1] was beaten. The latter, however, is standing for
the Assembly, the famous M. Barodet,[2] whose election
to the Assembly just extinct produced such a scandal,
having gallantly withdrawn to make room for him. But
M. Barodet has since begun to oppose another candi-
date, and a wiser man than himself, in another *arron-
dissement.* How the forthcoming elections will turn out
no man can tell, and I believe the oldest political observers decline to risk any prophecies. The results on
the thirtieth of January were in a measure a surprise—
they gave the Monarchists at once less to exult in and
less to raise the cry of alarm about than these gentlemen had—it may be said—hoped. It may be that in this
same direction those of ten days hence will be even
better.

M. Gambetta [3] has just been making an eloquent
speech at Lille—his age (he is less than forty) having
excluded him from the senatorship. It is all very reasonable as well as eloquent, save in so far as it commits
the liberal program to antagonism to the new Catholic
University.[4] M. Gambetta denounces in violent terms
the admission of the Church to a share in the superior
instruction.[5] This is a point on which many sagacious
Republicans distinctly differ with him—it has brought
down upon him, for instance, the animadversions of the
Journal des Débats, which for some time past has been
treating him with abundant respect. To give the Church
leave to bring up *émigrés,* as Gambetta says, within the
state, to form citizens who are no citizens, and with
whom it is a matter of conscience to plot and conspire

against it—this may be very fairly represented as suicidal. Certainly there is no such cruel knot for a liberal party to have to untie as the question how far it can afford to appear intolerant, and the history of Republicanism in France is associated with so many ugly doings against the Church, that the question is peculiarly difficult here. It should of course be settled in perfect indifference to the ironical cries of the Church party itself; but though M. Gambetta declares that it is a matter with which considerations of liberty and tolerance have nothing to do—a matter of simple self-preservation—it is inevitable that some people should ask themselves whether the remedy is not worse than the disease. If I were a Frenchman I am inclined to think that I should feel more at my ease in a republic in which the Catholic party was allowed to carry on, in competition with the Sorbonne and the Collège de France, as successful and satisfactory a university as it could, than in a republic in which it was silenced and muzzled and forced to disseminate its instruction through private channels. It is hard, indeed, to imagine a Catholic university, with the full light of our current audacity of opinion beating down upon it, proving very dangerous. I indulged, however, just above in a very fantastic hypothesis. Heaven forbid—for simple entertainment's sake—that anyone who has the good fortune not to be a Frenchman should become one, even in thought, at the present hour. They are a sadly perplexed people, and I find the spectacle of the various conflicting embodiments of opinion which I here and there encounter much more interesting than the monotonous interest of having a responsible bundle of doctrines and sticking to it. Without at all pleading guilty to the charge of that exaggeration of versatility known as being of the opinion of the last speaker, I never hear a political sympathy strongly expressed without desiring at least to understand it—to get inside of the speaker's mind, circumstances, and antecedents. The other day a lady was talking to me of a gentleman whom she had ceased for some time to see— he was so violent a Republican.[6] He had none but Republicans at his house, and they were all horrible people. "No French people," she added in a moment, "are Republicans—at least no one that anyone sees." This seemed to me in its way quite sublime, and it was certainly excusable to desire to pass half an hour in a place so warm and snug and free from uncomfortable drafts as this lady's moral consciousness. An evening or two later I was in a room into which M. Buffet presently entered, and a lady with whom I was talking made me turn and look at him. "I believe," she said in a moment, very softly and sweetly, "that M. Buffet is the best man on earth." Certainly if you don't dislike the vice-president of the Council very much, you will probably love him; but if, as an impartial observer, you happen to be looking at him in the flesh, you will probably feel a certain irritation at hearing him spoken of tenderly. Not that he is not very well worth turning round to look at, anywhere; but his physiognomy expresses the beau ideal of toughness.

He looks like a fine sixteenth-century print; his face, which is full of dignity and refinement, is, as it were, a masterly piece of wood engraving. Beneath the cut, on a scroll, in old, quaint letters, ought to be written—obstinacy. M. Buffet's countenance exhibits this quality in truly heroic proportions; and again, as I say, I should have been thankful for a glimpse of the intellectual economy of my companion, who found it so sympathetic. I do not know exactly what to say of a gentleman whom I lately encountered, and who, being a literary critic of much eminence, had for many years delighted me by his writings. On my asking how he felt about the elections—"Oh, it is done, this time, decidedly, it is done," he answered in the most mournful accents. "We are Americanizing! Yes, it's done." And he proceeded to affirm, with an air of dejection so profound, that the republican form was fatally different from those under which France had acquired her greatness, that I had not the heart to remind him of what his phrase, under the circumstances, lacked in perfect urbanity. I contented myself with suggesting that some of the forms under which France had grown great would make a rather ugly figure today.

I have just been looking through a new book by M. Émile de Girardin,[7] a heavy octavo of 750 pages, entitled *Grandeur ou Déclin de la France*. There is a great deal of good sense in it, and if there were more Frenchmen of this author's highly reasonable temper the future of France would be less problematical. M. de Girardin, who has always been before the public in

one way or another, has been more than once called a
turncoat and a weathercock, but he has really been
quite self-consistent, for his constant principle has been
to ask for all the liberty that was possible under the
circumstances. He glories in the fact that he has never
been an "irreconcilable"; he has accepted the situation
under every government, and exerted himself to get all
the good that was possible out of it. This long book—
which is but a collection of his newspaper articles of
the last two years, and which does not contain a single
word of sterile recrimination against Germany, or even
of acrimonious allusion—is an ardent appeal to his
countrymen to sink party differences in a frank acceptance of the Republic. It may be said that his demonstration of the issueless character of both monarchy
and empire is more successful than any insurance he
has to offer against the perils of that straining radi-
calism which the Republic carries in its flanks; but he
does not claim that the Republic is the millennium,
only that it is relative repose. Above all he wants things
settled upon their intrinsic merits, and not by party
considerations, and he is probably one of the few
Frenchmen who would have the courage to write, "If
such a prince is better for such an office than such a
radical, let us without hesitating take the prince; but
if such a radical is better than such a prince, let us
take the radical." But in truth, in France, when the
radical shall lie down with the prince, I imagine that
the millennium really will have arrived. M. de Girardin
has the further audacity to recommend forgiveness of

the Prussians—to deprecate, that is, in the strongest terms, all thoughts of a *revanche*. He hopes for a peaceful one someday, by diplomatic and equitable means, and meantime he wishes France to shake herself free of her military incubus. He deliberately entreats her to give up arming, and he maintains that if she does it Germany will be enchanted to do likewise. I do not know that he is absolutely right, but there is certainly something to be said in that sense. I have a suspicion, however, that M. de Girardin does not privately care for the *revanche* as much as a purely ideal patriotism would seem to recommend; his dream is to see France the greatest commercial and industrial country. The sanest men have their hobbies, and that of the editor of the *France* is that his country, if it only wills it, may become a great maritime power and cover the seas with her merchant fleets. Certainly there are things enough under the sun France can do, if she will only set her house in order and give her mind—her admirable mind —to them. I had marked as worth quoting a couple of extracts which M. de Girardin makes from two Bonapartist publications, but I have space only to allude to them. One of these volumes is by M. Georges Lachaud,[8] and it consists of an exemplification of the program contained in these words: "The condemnation of the French people to gaiety in perpetuity." "Persuaded as we are," says M. Georges Lachaud, on behalf of the Empire, "that a dictatorship alone, by disembarrassing the French people of its grave cares, can restore to it its lightness and its grace, we await with impatience the hour in which France will transfer to the shoulders of a master the burden that renders her thoughtful. Let our future master bring the 'imperial corruption' into honor again! And if ever his detractors accuse him of degrading the people, and bring forward to outrage him the old Roman device, *panem et circenses*, on that day the chief of the state may say with pride that he is really a great sovereign!" "The great duty of the Empire," M. Lachaud adds—and the formula seems to me an exquisite *trouvaille* (it is worthy to have been put into circulation by Napoleon III himself, who had a genius for the invention of phrases with just that sound)—"the great duty of the Empire is to *extirper le pessimisme.*" Delightful idea! But things are not looking well for M. Lachaud's optimism, and it seems as if he and his friends were more likely to be extirpated.

In the midst of her political turmoil Paris has had time to drop a sigh over the grave of Frédéric Lemaître, who died at a very advanced age a fortnight ago. The newspapers have been full of tributes to his memory, and his death following so close upon that of that other grotesquely aged veteran, Déjàzet, has been a piece of good luck for the anecdote mongers. I incline to think, from what I have heard and read of him, that he was one of the greatest of actors, but that he needed a great license, a great margin, to show his powers. The present generation had seen him—for poverty had repeatedly driven him back to the stage after the chill of age had settled upon him—but it did not know him. It is only our elders—those who remember Victor Hugo's *Marion Delorme* and *Ruy Blas* and Alexandre Dumas' *Anthony* as new pieces—that know him. He was formed by the passionate romantic drama that began its career in 1830. He was the actor for the time; he inspired Victor Hugo, and Victor Hugo inspired him in turn. He never succeeded at the Français —he was too fantastic and audacious—he played tragedy with a sense of humor. For an actor he grew old very young. He reminds one of what we hear of Garrick, in having had equal triumph in tragedy and comedy. The theater of our own day, with its relish for small, realistic effects, produces no more actors of those heroic proportions. The nearest approach to them is perhaps to be found in Got [9] at the Théâtre Français, who has an element of high fantasy, as those who have seen him in the curious revival of the medieval farce of *Maître Patelin* must remember. But Got is on the whole really a philosophic actor, and Frédéric Lemaître was an imaginative one. The ideal actor nowadays—the actor formed by Sardou and Dumas *fils* and Feuillet—is Worms of the Gymnase, who renders prose, not verse, and whose minute and exquisite strokes are like a masterly etching. But Frédéric Lemaître, as we see him in his *légende*, is like a huge, fantastic shadow, a moving silhouette, projected duskily against the wall from a glowing fire. The fire is the "romantic" movement of 1830.

H. JAMES, JR.
March 4, 1876

9

PARISIAN AFFAIRS

Letter from Henry James, Jr.

THE REPUBLIC IN THE HANDS OF REPUBLICANS—RAPID
SUCCESSION OF POLITICAL EVENTS—M. GAMBETTA'S
SAGACITY—DUMAS' NEW PLAY, "L'ÉTRANGÈRE"—MERITS
AND DEMERITS OF THE PERFORMANCE—THE CARNIVAL
IN PARIS

[FROM A REGULAR CORRESPONDENT OF THE "TRIBUNE"]

PARIS, Feb. 28, 1876.—That a large Republican
majority has been returned to the new Assembly, that
the Bonapartists have been (to all present appearance)
hopelessly beaten, that M. Buffet, in his appeal to four
electoral districts, has failed with a completeness which
leaves nothing to be desired, that the said M. Buffet
has sent in his resignation as vice-president of the
Council of Ministers, and that Marshal MacMahon has
accepted it, that the Conservatives in general, and
timid people in particular, profess themselves terribly
frightened, and that in fact the Funds have gone down,
and are staying down—all this, by the time these lines
reach you, will have become an old story, and will possibly have been superseded by events even more thrill-

ing. For the moment, however, here, this is thrilling enough—even for those who see no reason for being frightened except a deliberate preference for the tragic or pathetic state of mind. In the defeat of M. Buffet in particular, by the four constituencies to which he had presented himself, there has been something singularly complete and symmetrical—something, as I have seen it well observed, of that quality which we attribute to providential interposition. It is really a theme for the moralist. M. Buffet, for the present, retires to private life. When he emerges again, as a man of his tenacious instincts inevitably must, how will it stand with the Republic? Not so ill doubtless as the frightened people insist upon believing, nor so well perhaps as those who pin their faith upon the small radical leaven of the new Republican majority would fain proclaim on the house-tops. Without giving up everything for lost, or taking the fall of the Rentes too much to heart, or insisting to—*gagner la frontière*—if one has time, as one of the characters in *L'Étrangère* says—it may be affirmed that the situation is as serious as it has been for many a day. But it is serious in a good and healthy sense. The Republic is now for the first time in Republican hands, and it remains to be seen what they will make of it. The day of speeches and promises and generalities is over, and the day of political conduct has come. It entails a great responsibility, and it will be interesting to see how the party of M. Gambetta meet the occasion. In so far as they are the party of M. Gambetta the prospect is fair enough, for the conduct of their leader during the late campaign has been distinguished by moderation, tact, and extreme political sense. His split with the pure Radicals is now complete, and if he gets the start of them in the coming session, as there is no good reason why he should not, they will have lost their power to compromise him. His enemies affirm that he will throw off the mask and show himself as red as the reddest. I doubt it; he has been at too much trouble to put the mask on, and he has learned to wear it too well. He would want, if nothing else, to reap the crop of his discomfort. In the present situation of the Republican party there is certainly something inspiring if they will understand it—understand that they have just prejudices and damning associations to overcome, that the presumption is fairly enough against them, and that they are exceptionally bound to moderation, tact, and patience. Some people despair of their doing anything of the sort, others hope they will, others go so far as to believe they will. With a very little encouragement I shall feel like passing from the second to the third category. We shall not get that encouragement, however, from hearing Victor Hugo, as soon as the Senate opens, present a request for a universal amnesty. This performance will be a perfect specimen of the things which, under the circumstances, the new majority must on no account do.

If it is true that the country is going to the bad, and that the celebrated "era of revolutions" is again to open, people are beguiling the interval in such fashion as they may. A convenient sedative to suspense is found to be an evening at the Théâtre Français, where they are now playing Alexandre Dumas' long-expected drama *L'Étrangère*. Besides your evening, in this case you can get plenty to talk about afterward. The production of this piece has been the event of the winter. Besides its intrinsic importance, there were several accessory reasons for its attracting attention. It is the first play (if I am not mistaken) that Dumas has produced since his election to the Academy, as well as the first that he has presented to the Théâtre Français. The curiosity of the public, moreover, had been very skillfully stimulated, and the last rehearsal of the play had all the honors of a first representation. *L'Étrangère*, after all, has been but a moderate success—though, certainly, many a poor playwright would be enchanted that "moderation" should deal out his laurels and his percentage in this particular fashion. The great theater is crowded, and for the least little orchestra chairs you have to apply a week in advance. Nevertheless, the play is pronounced indifferent by some people, and shockingly bad by others. No one, as far as I have observed, has had the originality to call it good. I happened to hear it discussed, a few days since, among several gentlemen who are more or less of the same guild as its author, and it was as pretty a cutting up as one could desire to see.[1] The general verdict was that Alexandre Dumas has so much wind in his sails (from former successes) that he will float safely across his present shallows, but that his decline (since decline it is) will be cumulative; that another piece as bad as *L'Étrangère* will have much worse luck, and that the more gentle the public has been for the author hitherto, the more pitiless it will be when he begins to sink. Has he already begun to sink? I confess that *L'Étrangère* strikes me as a rather desperate piece of floundering in the dramatic sea. It is a long story, and I cannot pretend to relate it in detail. Suffice it that the Foreigner who gives its title to the piece, and who is played by that very interesting actress, Mme. Sarah Bernhardt,[2] is a daughter of our own democracy, Mrs. Clarkson by name. She explains, in the second act, by a mortal harangue—the longest, by the watch, I have ever listened to—that she is the daughter of a mulatto slave girl and a Carolinian planter. As she expresses it herself, "My mother was pretty: he remarked her; I was born of the remark." Mrs. Clarkson, however, has next to nothing to do with the action of the play, and she is the least successful figure that the author has ever drawn. Why she should be an American, why she should have Negro blood, why she should be the implacable demon that she is represented, why she should deliver the melodramatic and interminable tirade I have mentioned, why she should come in, why she should go out, why, in short, she should exist—all this is the perfection of mystery. She is like the heroine of an old-fashioned drama of the Boulevard du Crime who has strayed unwittingly into a literary work, in which she is out of time with all her companions. She is, on Dumas' part, an incredible error of taste. It must be confessed, however, that her entrance into the play has a masterly effectiveness. The whole first act indeed is an excellent start, though the goal is never really reached. As one of the characters says, we are *en pleine décomposition sociale*. The Duchess de Sept-Monts is giving a charity ball, and the circle of her particular intimates is collected about her in one of her apartments. The lady in question has been sold by her father, a retired tradesman of immense fortune, to a penniless and exhausted little rake, who, driven to bay by his creditors, has been delighted to raise money on his ducal title by the simple expedient of matrimony. Her father and her husband are present, and the conversation alights upon Mrs. Clarkson, the mysterious American, her beauty, her diamonds, her sinister reputation, her innumerable conquests, and her total absence of female friends. No respectable woman has ever entered her house or has ever received her. It so happens that the Duchess's father, her husband and her lover are all entangled in Mrs. Clarkson's toils, and these facts more or less explicitly transpire. The baleful beauty is moreover even now on the premises; she has been seen in the garden among the visitors present by right of having purchased their ticket—seen on the arm of the Duchess's lover (a lover who is as yet, I hasten to add, sincerely platonic). Abruptly the Duchess is approached by a servant with a card, which she reads in deep agitation. She writes a few words on another card and gives it to the footman; he goes off with it, and then she reads aloud to the company the contents of the first missive. Mrs. Clarkson requests

permission to be admitted to the salon in which the
Duchess sits apart with her intimates, there to receive
from the Duchess's own hands a cup of tea. In compensation, she offers to pay for her cup of tea the sum
of 25,000 francs, which the Duchess will make over to
the charity for which the ball has been given. At the
revelation of this audacity the little circle is aghast,
and demands with a single voice what the Duchess has
answered. The Duchess has answered that Mrs. Clarkson may be admitted if one of the gentlemen actually
about the hostess will go out, offer his arm, and conduct her into the ducal presence. There is a particular
silence—half-a-dozen gentlemen are present, but not
one of them moves. Finally the shaky, unclean little
Duke himself (admirably played by Coquelin) [3] stands
forth and declares that he will play the gallant part.
The announcement makes a great sensation, for it is
his presumed mistress that he proposes to introduce
to his wife. He departs and shortly afterward returns,
bearing Mrs. Clarkson on his arm, in all the effectiveness of the strange physiognomy and the fantastic
toilet of yellow and black which Mme. Sarah Bernhardt
has conferred upon her. "A cup!" shouts the outraged
Duchess, sticking to her bargain and nothing but her
bargain. I must not relate what follows. The real heroine of the play is Mlle. Croizette,[4] who played the
Duchess with a great deal of skill and with all that
strangely meretricious charm for which she is re-
nowned. She has one really magnificent scene—a scene
in which the ill-used (but on her own side by no means

unpeccant) heroine, the cup of whose disgust at her husband's turpitude is full, pours it all forth in rage and scorn upon his ignoble head. This is nature caught in the act—Mlle. Croizette's cries and gestures, the passionate reality of her imprecations, electrify the house. The author makes his duchess say things which have never before been said on the stage, but the artistic good faith of the actress carries them off.

I should mention that there is also a Mr. Clarkson in the play—a gentleman engaged in gold-washing in Utah, while his wife drinks tea at five thousand dollars the spoonful in Paris. Half the merit of this figure is with Febvre,[5] who represents it, and who, in particular, has dressed his Yankee with great felicity—quite in the occidental taste, and yet without the least exaggeration. On the whole, as I have said, *L'Étrangère* has been a disappointment, and it is unquestionably a very unsatisfactory piece of work for so clever a man as Dumas. It hangs very loosely together, and the story is both extremely improbable and profoundly disagreeable. Disagreeable, above all, for there is not a person in the play who is not, in one way or another, misbehaving grossly. Everyone is in the wrong, and the author most of all. And then his drama is saturated with that aroma of bad company and loose living which is the distinctive sign of M. Dumas' muse. This lady is afflicted with a congenital want of perception of certain rudimentary differences between the possible, for decent people, and the impossible. She has also on this occasion abused her characteristic privilege of indulging in pretentious tirades of the would-be philosophic order—explaining that love is physics and marriage is chemistry, &c.

It appears that for a number of weeks past we have been in Carnival. I confess that I never suspected it, and, by way of making up my arrears of perception of the subject, I went last night to the masked ball of the Opera. This was the only ball that the Opera, in its present gorgeous domicile, has offered. Half a dozen used to be given annually in the old opera house, but the present establishment considers this vulgar profusion beneath its dignity. It seems to me quite right, for, without making too much of the merits of the present structure, one may affirm that they are at least of a higher order than the laborious gambols of the rabble to show, last night, the privilege of dancing was by common consent surrendered. The crowd of spectators was enormous, but the maskers and dancers were woefully seedy and shabby. The *beaux jours* of masked revelry in Paris are evidently over. Peace to their ashes! The new Opera, arranged for the purpose as the French know how to arrange such things, made a superb ballroom, and Strauss's orchestra, on its immense platform, thundered away with an impressiveness which might have made the antics of dancers a trifle less dingy seem heroic. Behind the open stage the *foyer de la danse* was exhibited in a very effective manner. It is a kind of huge rococo boudoir, ornamented with medallions bearing portraits of all the great mistresses of the pirouette, from the Camargo to Carlotta

Grisi.[6] It was filled with plants and grassy banks, among which you might fancy the ghosts of these departed sylphs coming down in their short-skirted shrouds to execute a spectral ballet, and at its back was a great wall of plate glass, which reflected the whole hall and doubled its extent. This was a good deal more than enough, however, for a masked ball at a theater begets, as Hamlet says, a pestilent congregation of vapors. As I came away betimes, and saw the great mounted cuirassiers stationed in the darkness along the approaches, they seemed in their immobility to have something refreshingly severe and monumental.

HENRY JAMES, JR.

March 25, 1876

10

PARISIAN TOPICS

Letter from Henry James, Jr.

THE RECEPTION OF JOHN LEMOINNE AT THE ACADEMY
—HIS CHARACTERISTICS AS A JOURNALIST—THE VARI-
ABLE MERITS OF ACADEMICIANS—M. GÉRÔME'S "CHAR-
IOT RACE"—PRESIDENT LINCOLN AND STONEWALL JACK-
SON DRAMATIZED—VICTOR TISSOT ON THE PRUSSIANS

[FROM A REGULAR CORRESPONDENT OF THE "TRIBUNE"]

PARIS, March 10.—Except [for] the assembling of
the Senate and the Chamber I can think of no event
of importance of recent occurrence here save the reception of M. John Lemoinne [1] at the Academy, which
took place a week since. M. John Lemoinne is the
eminent journalist—the bright particular star of the
Débats—and journalism has received in his person at
the hands of the Academy a compliment of which, if
she particularly desires to, she may be proud. It was
a proud day at least for the *Journal des Débats*. John
Lemoinne replaces Jules Janin,[2] who spent forty years
in the "basement," as they call it, of that honorable
sheet—turned off every Monday during that period
the dramatic feuilleton which graces the bottom of its

otherwise somewhat austere first two pages. He pronounced the customary eulogy of his departed con-
frère, and M. Cavillier-Fleury replied to him at very
great length with a eulogy of himself, M. Cavillier-
Fleury being the principal literary critic of the *Journal des Débats*. It was therefore, for this journal, quite
a *fête de famille*. M. John Lemoinne is a very clever
man; he possesses in perfection the French "art of
saying," and if the Academy was designed simply to
represent good writing, he has an eminent claim to a
place in it. (It is singular, by the way, that M. John
Lemoinne should, as a writer, be of so pure a French
strain. He was born in England, and, in a measure,
educated there, and he speaks our language irreproach-
ably.) If, however, to reward good thinking and good
feeling is a part of the Academy's mission,[3] M. Lemoinne's right of entrance does not seem so unques-
tionable. Brilliant, incisive, and trenchant as he always
is, I have never been able to resist the feeling that there
is something very dry and sterile in his political criticism. To say acrimonious and contemptuous things in
a masterly manner appears to be the sum of his ambition. He is essentially what the French call a *frondeur*
—a faultfinder; his criticism is always restrictive and
denunciatory, never suggestive or inspiring, and he
lacks supremely Matthew Arnold's famous requisite of
"sweetness." This is the greater pity, as he has evidently plenty of "light." He seems to proceed by fits
of irritation. He appears in the *Débats* not daily, but
at intervals; suddenly darts forth, whirling his sling

and letting fly his sharp flints. When he has quite darkened the air with them he retires to his tent—feeling better himself for the time, I hope—to await a fresh re-exasperation of his wrath. It is all nervous, capricious, splenetic. M. John Lemoinne's chief stock in trade is his peculiarly insidious hatred of England, and, indeed, during the past winter, exciting as the political situation has been, it is only the perfidy of Albion that has been able to rouse him to utterance. At the time of the purchase of the Khedive's shares he came out, as the phrase is, very strong, and produced two or three articles in which the expression of withering enmity could not have been surpassed. England, for M. Lemoinne, is a shabby country at the best, but her unpardonable sin was her failure to come to the rescue of France when the latter was bleeding to death in the grip of Prussia—her "standing watching us stretched on the earth like gladiators." And yet even this is not sufficient to account for such a perennial freshness of hostility. The reader cannot rid himself of a feeling that M. John Lemoinne is avenging a personal injury; where does the shoe pinch, he wonders; whom has he in his mind—*à qui en veut-il?* These conjectures are probably fantastic, and they are certainly vain.

M. LEMOINNE AND THE ACADEMY [4]

The fact remains, however, that M. Lemoinne's England is very much an affair of his imagination; it is, as the London *Times* said the other day, an *article de*

Paris. I may add that the sturdiest Anglo-Saxon must have had last week a kindly feeling for the new Academician, in seeing him undertake the heroic task of eulogizing (I was going to say apologizing for) Jules Janin. M. John Lemoinne did his best, but unless I am very much mistaken one hears the creaking of the pump. There have been many strange Academicians, but I think there has been none quite so strange as the dramatic critic of the *Débats.* There have been Academicians whose literary titles were of the slenderest, and who were admitted for reasons of state—thinly disguised motives of convenience and propriety; there have been—heaven knows!—dull, dreary, insipid Academicians, authors of classical, respectable, unreadable prose and verse. There have also been flimsy and futile Academicians, whose literature was of a vaporous and imponderable sort. But there was none before M. Jules Janin who had erected futility into a system and raised flimsiness to a fine art.

There are writers in whom mannerism has gone very far, but there are none in whom it has become the all in all to the same degree as in Janin. His mannerism in his later years attained the proportions of a monstrosity. Such a shuffling away of substance, such a juggling with thought, partook really of the nature of the magical. He was the great master of the type of criticism that speaks of everything but the subject, and that spins its phrases faster in proportion as it has less and less to say. Janin ended very early by having nothing in life to say, and the rattle and clatter he made in saying it was to all healthy intellectual men the most intolerable noise conceivable. If the Academy has any meaning, one would say that its meaning should be exactly that its honors are not for writers of the Janin family. But has the Academy any meaning? Two or three incidents have lately occurred which make the inquiry proper. The most striking was certainly the admission among the sacred party, last spring, of Alexandre Dumas *fils*. M. Dumas is supremely clever, and he has composed dramas which it is impossible, on certain sides, too highly to admire; but it seems to me that he has about as much business in the Academy as in the Cabinet of the Emperor of China. He is a man with a fixed idea—a monomaniac. He can see nothing in life but the "unfortunate" woman; she is the pivot of his imagination—all his inspiration, his allusions and metaphors are drawn from her. If the Academy were an intellectual asylum, with wards, cells, and keepers, M. Dumas might very well appeal to its hospitality; but as it is, there is something grotesque in his presence there. The prime duty of the Academy ought to be to distinguish between the cracked vessel and the sound; [5] and it seems to me that if she had observed this duty, she would have said to Jules Janin and Alexandre Dumas, alike (dissimilar in talent as they are), that they were welcome to be clever, and popular, and brilliant, but that they were made of precisely the stuff she could not wear—they were deformed, erratic, mistaken. "Here is a certain straight line," she should have said, "you and I can never be on the same side of it."

MR. STEWART'S ART PURCHASE

I saw a few days since a large picture lately finished by M. Gérôme [6] for the gentleman in New York whom I mentioned some time since as the purchaser of Meissonier's "1807," and such reasons as made it opportune to allude to that work apply in the present case. They apply, however, with less force, for in Gérôme's "Chariot Race" (as I suppose the picture is called), Mr. A. T. Stewart has made a less brilliant acquisition. On the other hand, the picture is not on exhibition. It is a capital example of the artist's archaeological skill—though it would require a specialist to determine, on this line, its triumphs and its shortcomings. What the ordinary observer sees is that the painter has mastered a vast amount of curious detail, and after all, unless the ghost of some old Roman man about town comes back for the purpose, I do not see who is to prove that M. Gérôme's ingenious reconstruction is either a good likeness of the actual scene or a poor one. I believe that the eminent architect, M. Viollet-le-Duc (who, by the way, though lavishly patronized by the Empire, has lately come out as a thoroughgoing radical), worked with the painter in Rome at the plan of the picture. It represents what I take to be the Circus Maximus, on a day of high festivity; behind rise the towers, pal-

aces, and terraces of the Palatine, and into the distance
stretches away the vast ellipse of the arena. The spectators are embanked above it in high, steep, parti-col-
ored slopes, the sunshine pouring over them—or over
those that we see—and touching the reds and yellows
of their dresses into gaudiness. Down the center of
the circus runs a long, narrow platform, covered with
brazen monuments and columns, and making at each
extremity the corner which the chariots are to turn.
They have reached the end which is presented to the
spectators of the picture, and they are in the act of
rounding the brazen cape, from which a great por-
phyry column rises like a lighthouse. They are eight
in number—as one distinguishes them among their
clouds of dust—and each has three horses abreast. It
is a fierce *mêlée* of beasts, men, and wheels; the strug-
gle and confusion are powerfully expressed, and the
horses and chariots painted with that hard, consummate finish characteristic of the author. The coloring
of the picture, meanwhile, is not that to which Gérôme
has accustomed us; it has a certain anomalous crudity
and an abuse of bricklike tones. It is evident, however,
that this is perfectly calculated. The painter has wished
to represent the full glare of sunshine on bedizened and
gilded surfaces, on stained and painted walls, and on
garments in which the mingled and complex tones of
the modern costume were unknown. He has an immense
expanse of functionaries in one section of the auditory
—senators possibly—draped in pure vermilion.

AN AMERICAN MELODRAMA

The adventurous American in Paris at the present moment is deriving much entertainment from going to see the highly successful melodrama of the *Chevaliers de la Patrie*, at the Théâtre Historique. I say "adventurous," because the theater in question is very far off, and, though of splendid aspect and proportion, much frequented by that class of amateurs who find the suspense of the entr'actes intolerable without the beguilement of an orange. The drama in question treats bravely of the American civil war, and the "chevaliers" from whom it takes its name are Abraham Lincoln and Stonewall Jackson. It is in no less than eight acts, but I sat to the end, for it is a most exhilarating affair. The author, one M. Delpit,[7] is, I believe, by birth a Louisianian. He evidently "knows better," but he knows that his audience does not, and he gives them their money's worth of local color. In the first act the greater part of the *dramatis personae* are assembled on a steamboat on the Potomac, and they all come to the side of the vessel and narrate their histories to the audience. Meanwhile the steamboat is racing with a craft of an opposition line, and the captain has formally announced that his boat must win the race or blow up. One or other of the boilers must burst—they can only hope it will be the other. The passengers exclaim in chorus, "All right!" and await further developments. At last the rival steamboat comes alongside, and, after a moment of painful suspense, explodes.

"It's the other!" cry the passengers, and continue their promenade on the deck. The sequel is worthy of this beginning, but I cannot begin to unweave its tangled web. Abraham Lincoln is ever administering justice in one of the saloons of the White House, like a primitive chieftain under the spreading oak. The White House, indeed, appears to open out in the rear into the forest primeval. The scene is of course in a high degree farcical, but the actor who represents Mr. Lincoln has succeeded in making up his head into a very tolerable likeness of the original. Then we are transported to the southern army, in which two gallant young Frenchmen have come to seek commissions, and [are] introduced to Stonewall Jackson and the famous cavalry chieftain, Stuart. This, of course, furnishes the opportunity for a very dramatic contrast—Jackson sitting reading the Bible on one side of the stage, Stuart draining his glass on the other, and the southern army displayed in the background. Stuart proposes to give a fête in the evening, but Jackson piously protests. Stuart, however, insists. Jackson goes off in sorrow, if not in anger, and the fête—consisting of a dozen Negro minstrels and as many ballet girls—is promptly put forward. It is interrupted, however, by the return of Jackson on a litter, fresh from the field of battle, and mortally wounded. During the fête a battle has been raging, at which Stuart's attendance appears to have been deemed superfluous. Jackson, in his death agony, struts and stamps about the stage, and requests the two French officers to repair straightway to Washington

and kidnap Mr. Lincoln. This they proceed to do in
the next act; but Wilkes Booth—whose name has been
altered by the censorship—comes very near being beforehand with them. They are all baffled, however, by
the sublimity of Mr. Lincoln's conversation, and the
curtain falls upon the reunion of the French officers
and their sweethearts in one of the parlors of the White
House, where the President fraternally blesses them.

There is a certain analogy between this brave burlesque and the lively travesty of actual things presented in M. Victor Tissot's [8] second volume on his adventures in Germany. The book has been out but a few
days, and it is already in its eighth edition. M. Victor
Tissot is the author of the *Voyage au Pays des Milliards*, which was published a few months since, and is
now in its twenty-second edition. He at present gives
a sequel, *Les Prussiens en Allemagne*, which I suppose
will gain the same distinction as its predecessor—that
of being placed under an interdict in Berlin. This last
circumstance raises the one presumption in favor of
M. Tissot's veracity. He is exceedingly clever, admirably observant, and his Teutophobia, as an exhibition
of vivacity and energy, is really very fine. But, like M.
Lemoinne's England, his Germany is quite an *article
de Paris*. I heard a gentleman of Germanic sympathies [9]
characterize an impertinent fable the other day as *du
Tissot tout pur*, and certainly M. Tissot's reader
largely repunctuates his pages with interrogation
marks. He should remember the proverb that he who

wishes to prove too much proves nothing. The French, they say, are beginning to study Germany, but they had better not take M. Tissot's volumes for their textbooks.

HENRY JAMES, JR.
April 1, 1876

Parisian Topics

11

ART AND LETTERS IN PARIS

Letter from Henry James, Jr.

THE PARISIAN ART MARKET—DECAMPS' DISTINCTIVE
MERITS—MARILHAT'S PAINTINGS—ORIENTAL SKETCHES
ABUNDANT—MEISSONIER'S "READER"—THE FLOODS IN
THE SEINE—CURRENT LITERATURE

[FROM A REGULAR CORRESPONDENT OF THE "TRIBUNE"]

PARIS, March 21.—In default of any topic with a
high interest of what the French call "actuality," there
is something to say today about pictures. I have recently seen a good many; but heaven forbid I should
speak of them all! I have seen several, however, the
reappearance of which in the art market is worth commemorating, and may interest those people at least
who keep a record of such matters. Two important
collections of French pictures, formed many years ago
in Holland, are about to be dispersed in consequence
of the death of their owners, and have of course been
sent to Paris to be disposed of. This operation is to
take place a month hence at the Hôtel Drouot, and
meanwhile one seems to hear the meditative rattle of
coin in the sidepockets of amateurs not compelled, like

most newspaper correspondents, to be purely platonic.
I had the pleasure, the other day, of having an an-
ticipatory view of these two collections, which are not
yet on exhibition, and it yielded me much entertainment. Part of the entertainment was perhaps independ-
ent of the rigidly intrinsic merit of Meissonier and Decamps,[1] and consisted in lounging upon an ottoman
in a quiet room in an establishment in which the effective presentation of works of art has itself been raised
to a fine art, and seeing the gems of the series I mention plucked forth from an adjoining place of deposit and arrayed before me in skillful juxtaposition.
They certainly order this matter better in France than
anywhere in the world. A catalogue of each of the collections of which I speak has been put forward, illustrated by etchings from eminent hands, many of which
are admirable—so much so that people of modest as-
pirations, possessing the catalogue, may almost con-
sole themselves for being unlikely ever to possess any
of the works it describes. Among these there are two
or three charming Decamps and a couple of small but
superlative Meissoniers. Decamps is a painter of whom
I never tire, and one of the very few French artists in
whom, in the long run, one finds it possible to take a
sentimental pleasure, counting Delacroix, Millet, and
Rousseau [2] as the others. He is not so pure an original
as they, but like them he has an element of magic, of
independence of fancy—the precious something that
gives its highest value to a work of art that can be
learned in no school, and in its absence replaced by

no amount of practice. If practice could give it, Meissonier, Gérôme, and two or three of their supremely clever *confrères* ought to be rich in it; but in fact these gentlemen only prove that it is possible to go a good way without it. One of the specimens of Decamps is a small picture of a little peasant girl sitting under a tree in springtime, when the leaves above her are yet sparse, but the grass around her thick-strewn with anemones, and thrusting a great slice of the bread and butter with which she is besmearing her infant lips at a little white kid, who stands beside her. The subject is not heroic, and to call the scene pastoral, even, seems an exaggeration of its pretensions. But it is truly exquisite, and the landscape, beyond the figures, which are immediately in front, and in shadow, melts away into soft Italian crags and undulations, and glows with silver light. No painter plays with effects of light so delicately, and on the whole so unerringly, as Decamps. He shrinks from none of the atmospheric mysteries and complexities. He may easily be accused, of course, of playing too much, and be reminded that, according to the canons which have come into fashion of recent years, to play in a picture, to disport oneself, *dissiper*, is very nearly as wicked as to play on a Sunday—that a picture is indeed a kind of concentrated Sunday, a transported battleground of right and wrong, a deadly, solemn, and responsible thing. He will have, however, always, even in his most criminal aberrations, a good many admirers among the people who cannot help believing that the great charm of art is in its being a

change from life, and not a still narrower consciousness
of it, and who, even if he were a less brilliant genius,
would prize in Decamps his strong expression of this
sentiment. Another example of the same painter is a
picture of a couple of Italian *pifferari,* piping before
an image of the Madonna, in the close, hot streets of
some little southern city. It is a masterpiece as regards
the treatment of reflected lights, for there are none
other. The yellow afternoon sunshine, confined till it
grows thick, as it were, between walls of moldering
travertine reflected upon one, and thence reflected back
upon another, and broken and mixed with vague,
brown shadows, is here represented with admirable
verity. Anyone who has walked in the streets of small
Italian towns late in the long summer days will particularly relish this little picture. Such an observer will
seem to feel the warm, dead air again, and in the places
on which his eyes lingered, all the mellow—the almost
golden—dreariness.

A painter whom I always meet with pleasure, though
unfortunately one meets him but seldom, as he died
many years since, prematurely, before the list of his
works had grown long, is Marilhat, the precursor of
the innumerable tribe of clever Frenchmen who during
the last twenty years have "exploited" the Orient. I
do not know what Marilhat [3] would have been doing
now if he had lived to our own day; but coming when
he did, and stopping when he did, he has a charm of
which we must give him all the credit. It is an unhappy
thing in France, that as soon as an individual makes

a hit, in a certain line, in any of the arts, he immediately, and in spite of himself, founds a school—calls into activity a multitude of other persons who forthwith proceed to "do" that particular thing; to manufacture it, to elaborate the apparatus and perfect the system, so that it may be turned off in large quantities. The discovery by Delacroix and Decamps, forty years ago, that the bazaars of Cairo and Constantinople afforded a harvest of picturesque subjects is an excellent case in point. It took a little while for the movement to spread, and Marilhat, coming first, at his leisure, is fresh, charming, and sincere. Marilhat's natural refinement, his agreeable fancy, his simple and skillful touch, are capitally illustrated in an extremely beautiful picture which I the other day had before me—a great group of cedars perched on a huge, picturesque embankment of masonry, above a fountain, with a group of camel drivers and their beasts resting in the shade. It is the old East—the East of forty years ago, before the era of steamboats on the Nile and the British purchase of the Khedive's shares; [4] and there is in particular a certain old white-walled castle in the middle distance, which, with its faint gleams and its vague shadows, is alone, in vulgar parlance, worth the price of the picture. But after Marilhat came the troop among whom Gérôme is easily chief, and who have ransacked and rifled the oriental world of the uttermost vestige of its mystery. The trick has been learned, the recipe has been copied, passed through ten thousand hands. For some people the absolutely mechanical

cleverness of Gérôme has produced, as regards the
East, a complete disenchantment. The worst of all this
in France is that the secondary people, the imitators,
the school, the *queue*, are generally so odiously clever
that to a certain extent they challenge comparison with
their betters.

The collections I have mentioned contain two extraordinary little pictures by Meissonier—minute masterpieces each. I did not rank Meissonier just now among
the French painters I much care for; but there is none
we much more greatly admire. One of the diminutive
panels I mention represents a couple of medieval *Lands-
knechts*—a battered and grizzled old veteran, seated
against a wall, and a companion standing beside him.
This younger man, with his broad, round, densely-
curled head, his widely divided eyes, his short, narrow
beard, his hard, good-humored face, the perfection of
the choice of his type as an adjunct to a dented cuirass
and a pair of faded red velvet sleeves, is beyond all
praise. He is as solid and complete as if we had heard
him whistling while he polished his battered breast-
plate. An even greater triumph is the other picture,
which is famous under the title of "The Reader." Ah!
what a reader! He is a man of forty, clad in a red
velvet gown of the sixteenth century, sitting upright
in a shallow armchair, which supports his elbows, and
holding open, with the most delicate and sympathetic
fingers, a goodly little volume of the period, upon
which his intelligent brow is bent with a slight, pleasur-
able contraction, while his bearded lips are vaguely

pushed forward. Here is much in little, if there ever was—life, thought, history, dignity, culture, all condensed into the expression of a figure which you need a magnifying glass to look at properly. There could not be more of it if it were six feet high, and we could not believe more thoroughly in his admirable red velvet gown (it is hard to think that something fine did not pass out of human character when gentlemen used to wear such garments) if we had been his *valet de chambre*, and helped him to put it on. The head is to some extent a portrait of the artist.

Of the various pictures which I saw in combination with these, I have left myself no space to speak; well-chosen specimens as they each were, they formed a very honorable and brilliant summary of the French school—exclusive of its landscapists. There were, in particular, some admirable examples of the cattle-painter Brascassat,[5] who is little known in America, but who seems to me to handle his bulls and oxen in a much grander fashion than Rosa Bonheur. He has a striking resemblance to Paul Potter.[6] Let me commemorate also a couple of pictures by a young man named Baillet,[7] a pupil of Breton, the painter of fish-wives and harvest women, half bovine, half statuesque. M. Baillet is almost as good as his master, and the day he becomes quite as good he will be better. One of the subjects of which I speak—a group of peasant women washing clothes in some fresh-water pools near the sea, in the early twilight—is a very noble performance, and displays a union of imagination and self-control which

speaks well for the artist's future. It may be expected
to make an impression in the forthcoming Salon. I can
also not deny myself the satisfaction of turning a compliment to a young Italian painter, Boldini [8] by name,
for an admirable work to which, in my extreme relish
for it, I lately paid more than one visit. (The picture
in question, I must hasten to add, is, like others to
which I have had the honor of alluding, the property
of Mr. A. T. Stewart. I feel, in this connection, like
the cat in the fairy tale, pointing out the possessions
of the Marquis of Carabas.) My compliment to M.
Boldini, to be in keeping, should be flowery and cere-
monious, like the diction of the last century. He is the
most skillful among the little band of Italian painters
which has come into being within a few years past, with
powder and brocade, rococo fountains, sedan chairs,
and poodles for their especial inspiration. It is a sort
of neo-Watteau movement, and its obvious reproach
is that of triviality. Its equally obvious charm is that
it is irresistibly entertaining; it has a naïveté, a good
faith, a light jocularity quite distinct from the stale,
skeptical cleverness which characterizes so much French
art. M. Boldini's picture represents a corner of the
park at Versailles under Louis XVI. A sedan chair
containing a fine lady, escorted by several fops and
élégantes, has been deposited, while the carriers stand
resting, beneath a great wall of horse chestnut trees.
Nearby is a fountain and a couple of statues, and
where the horse chestnuts stop a broad cedar spreads
itself into the brilliant summer light. The figures are

very small—they belong to the class of what the French call little *bonshommes;* but their animation, expressiveness, and grace, the shimmer of their brocades and velvets, the gleam of their tense silk stockings, the way they hollow their backs and turn out their toes, are all extraordinary and delightful. The artist has a real divination of the costume of the time and the way it must have been worn. His great triumph here, however, has been his landscape—his great mass of verdure, and his dazzling, almost blinding summer light. This is so intense that in spite of its immense quantity of green, the picture is almost too white. But as a representation of objects shining and glowing in the open air, and as an almost childishly irreflective piece of fantasy, the work is a singular success.

In saying that there were just now no Parisian "actualities" of the first importance, I may seem to have slighted the overflow of the Seine, which has lately given Paris and its neighborhood plenty to talk about. The waters, moreover, are now fast subsiding, and the subject is a painful one, owing to the suffering and injury inflicted upon the poor people who form almost exclusively the population of the flooded quarters. Both up and down the river, outside of the center of Paris, everything habitable has been knee-deep in the water. I took a long walk the other night along the quays, past Notre Dame and the Jardin des Plantes, to see the immersion of Bercy. Since 1848 the river had not been so high, but its present condition, like a great many painful and cruel things, was extremely picturesque.

In the city it has been for a fortnight as big as a young Mississippi—doubling its apparent breadth from quay to quay, hiding the arches of the bridges up to the keystone, lifting up its barges and floating baths and swimming schools into unprecedented intimacy with the basements of the houses, and keeping half the *badauds*—the Paris cockneys—hanging all day over the parapets to watch a new centimeter disappear on the painted scale. Poor Bercy, in the sparsely illuminated darkness, looked like a little prosaic Venice, with boats paddling about in the streets and Parisian lamp posts rising out of muddy lagoons.

The only literary event of first-rate importance that has occurred in Paris during the winter has been the publication of Taine's *Ancien Régime*, of which, at the time, I made mention. In so sterile a season I suppose that the appearance in the last number of the *Revue des Deux Mondes* of the first installment of Ernest Renan's [9] *Souvenirs d'Enfance* may be spoken of as a salient event. The article appears to have attracted much attention, but to have caused some disappointment. It consists of two parts—a few pages of personal reminiscence by M. Renan himself, and a narrative taken down—with considerable embellishment—from the lips of his mother. The story is tame and of slender significance; but M. Renan's own memoirs are enchanting. His touch is more exquisite, his style more magical, surely, than any others of the day. The death of Daniel Stern (Mme. d'Agoult) [10] and that of Mme. Louise Colet [11] may also be spoken of as literary incidents. Mme. d'Agoult was a serious writer and Mme. Colet a light one, but both ladies had had beauty and adventures. Of these adventures the Abbé Liszt was the hero in one case, and Alfred de Musset in the other. I saw quoted the other day from Mme. d'Agoult a felicitous sentence: "An agreeable mind is a mind that is affirmative only in the measure strictly necessary." This dictum is characteristic of a writer who was also a very skillful *maîtresse de salon*. Mme. Colet never said anything so good as that. Some years ago, when Mme. Sand published her very ill-advised *Elle et Lui*, and Paul de Musset (the brother of the presumptive original of the hero) retorted with *Lui et Elle*, Mme. Colet cried like Correggio, "*Anch' io son pittore!*" and put forth a tale entitled *Lui*, the purpose of which was to prove, as I remember it, that she used to roam in the Bois de Boulogne in the small hours of the night in a low-necked dress, while "He," roaming hand in hand with her, showered kisses upon her shoulders. "Orpheus and the Bacchantes" these contributions to erotic history were happily called. Poor Orpheus!

HENRY JAMES, JR.

April 22, 1876

29 Rue de Luxembourg.

12

CHARTRES PORTRAYED [1]

Letter from Henry James, Jr.

BRILLIANT WEATHER IN PARIS—PRELIMINARIES OF A
DAY'S EXCURSION—IMPRESSIVENESS OF THE CATHEDRAL
AT CHARTRES—GENERAL ASPECT OF THE TOWN—
QUAINTNESS OF ITS SOCIAL LIFE

[FROM A REGULAR CORRESPONDENT OF THE "TRIBUNE"]

PARIS, April 9.—The spring in Paris, since it has
fairly begun, has been enchanting. The sun and the
moon have been blazing in emulation, and the difference between the blue sky of day and of night has been
as slight as possible. There are no clouds in the sky,
but there are little thin green clouds, little puffs of raw,
tender verdure, caught and suspended upon the
branches of the trees. All the world is in the streets;
the chairs and tables which have stood empty all winter before the café doors are at a premium; the theaters
have become intolerably close—the puppet shows in
the Champs Élysées are the only form of dramatic entertainment which seems consistent with the season. By
way of doing honor, at a small cost, to this ethereal
mildness, I went out the other day to the ancient town

of Chartres, where I spent several hours of the purest felicity. Pure felicity, in this hard world, always deserves to be recorded, and I cannot deny myself the pleasure of commemorating my admiration of one of the most beautiful churches in France. If one has not been traveling for a long time, there is, to an appreciative mind, a sort of intoxication in the mere fact of changing his place, and if one does so on a lovely spring day, under picturesque circumstances, the satisfaction is at its highest. To this perhaps rather frivolous emotion I must confess myself extremely susceptible, and the effect of it was to send me down to Chartres in a shamelessly optimistic state of mind. I was so prepared to be entertained and pleased with everything that it is only a mercy that the Cathedral happens to be a really fine building. If it had not been, I should still have admired it inordinately and rendered myself guilty of heaven knows what unpardonable aesthetic error. But I am almost ashamed to say how soon my entertainment began. It began, I think, with my hailing a little open carriage on the boulevard and causing myself to be driven to the Western Railway station—away across the river, up the Rue Bonaparte, of art-student memories, and along the big, straight Rue de Rennes to the Boulevard Montparnasse. Of course, at this rate, by the time I reached Chartres—the journey is of a couple of hours—I had almost drained the cup of pleasure. But it was replenished at the station, at the buffet, from the very good bottle of wine I drank with my breakfast. Here, by the way,

is another excellent excuse for being enchanted with
any day's excursion in France—wherever you are, you
may breakfast well. There may, indeed, if the station
is very small, be no buffet; but if there is a buffet, you
may be sure that civilization—in the persons of a sympathetic young woman in a well-made black dress, and
a rapid, zealous, grateful waiter—presides at it. It was
quite the least, as the French say, that after my breakfast I should have thought the Cathedral, as I saw it
from the foot of the steep hill on which the town stands,
rising high above the clustered houses, and seeming to
make of their red-roofed agglomeration a mere pedestal
for its immense beauty, promised remarkably well. You
see it so as you emerge from the station, and then, as
you climb slowly into town, you lose sight of it. You
perceive Chartres to be a rather shabby little *ville de
province,* with a few sunny, empty open places, and
crooked, shady streets, in which two or three times you
lose your way, until at last, after more than once catch-
ing a glimpse, high above some slit between the houses,
of the clear gray towers shining against the blue sky,
you push forward again, risk another short cut, turn
another interposing corner, and stand before the goal
of your pilgrimage.

I spent a long time looking at Chartres Cathedral;
I revolved around it, like a moth around a candle; I
went away and I came back; I chose twenty different
standpoints; I observed it during the different hours of
the day, and saw it in the moonlight as well as the sun-

shine. I gained, in a word, a certain sense of familiarity with it; and yet I despair of giving any very coherent account of it. Like most French cathedrals, it rises straight out of the street, and it is without that setting of turf and trees and deaneries and canonries which contribute so largely to the impressiveness of the great English churches. Thirty years ago a row of old houses was glued to its base and made their back walls of its sculptured sides. These have been plucked away, and, relatively speaking, the church is fairly isolated. But the little square that surrounds it is regretfully narrow, and you flatten your back against the opposite houses in the vain attempt to stand off and survey the towers. The proper way to look at the towers would be to go up in a balloon and hang poised, face to face with them, in the blue air. There is, however, perhaps an advantage in being forced to stand so directly under them, for this position gives you an overwhelming impression of their height. I have seen, I suppose, churches as beautiful as this one, but I do not remember ever to have been so touched and fascinated by architectural beauty. The endless upward reach of the great west front, the clear, silvery tone of its surface, the way a few magnificent features are made to occupy its vast, serene expanse, its simplicity, majesty, and dignity— these things crowd upon one's sense with an eloquence that one must not attempt to translate into words. The impressions produced by architecture lend themselves as little to interpretation by another medium as those produced by music. Certainly there is something of the beauty of music in the sublime proportions of the façade of Chartres.

The doors are rather low, as those of the English cathedrals are apt to be, but (standing three together) are set in a deep framework of sculpture—rows of arching grooves, filled with admirable little images, standing with their heels on each other's heads. The church as it now exists, except the northern tower, dates from the middle of the thirteenth century, and these closely packed figures are full of the grotesqueness of the period. Above the triple portals is a vast round-topped window, in three divisions, of the grandest dimensions and the stateliest effect. Above this window is a circular window of immense circumference, with a double row of sculptured spokes radiating from its center and looking on its great lofty field of stone, as expansive and symbolic as if it were the wheel of Time itself. Higher still is a little gallery with a delicate balustrade, supported on a beautiful cornice and stretching across the front from tower to tower; and above this is a range of niched statues of kings—fifteen, I believe, in number. Above the statues is a gable, with an image of the Virgin and Child on its front, and another of Christ on its apex. In the relation of all these parts there is such a spaciousness and harmony that while on the one side the eye rests on a great many broad stretches of naked stone, there is no approach on the other to overprofusion of detail. The little gallery that I have spoken of, beneath the statues of the kings, had for me a peculiar charm. Unavailable, at its tremendous altitude, for other purposes, it seemed fantastically intended for the little images to step down and walk about upon. When the great façade begins to glow in the late afternoon light, you can imagine them strolling up and down their long balcony in couples, pausing with their elbows on the balustrade, resting their stony chins in their hands, and looking out, with their little blank eyes, on the great view of the old French monarchy they once ruled, and which now has passed away. The two great towers of the Cathedral are among the noblest of their kind. They rise in solid simplicity to about as great a height as the eye often troubles itself to travel, and then, suddenly, they begin to execute a magnificent series of feats in architectural gymnastics. This is especially true of the northern spire, which is a late creation, dating from the sixteenth century. The other is relatively quiet; but its companion is a sort of tapering bouquet of sculptured stone. Statues and buttresses, gargoyles, arabesques, and crockets pile themselves in successive stages, until the eye loses the sense of everything but a sort of architectural lacework. The pride of Chartres, after its front, is the two portals of its transepts—great dusky porches, in three divisions, covered with more images than I have space to talk about. Wherever you look, along the sides of the church, a time-worn image is niched or perched. The face of each flying buttress is garnished with one, with the features quite melted away.

The inside of the Cathedral corresponds in vastness and grandeur to the outside—it is the perfection of

Gothic in its prime. But I looked at it rapidly, the place
was so intolerably cold. It seemed to answer one's query
of what becomes of the winter when the spring chases it
away. The winter hereabouts has sought an asylum in
Chartres Cathedral, where it has found plenty of room
and may reside in a state of excellent preservation until
it can safely venture abroad again. I thought I had
been in cold churches before, but the thought had been
an injustice to the temperature of Chartres. The nave
was full of the little padded chairs of the Chartres
bourgeoisie, whose faith, I hope for their comfort, is of
the good old red-hot complexion. In a higher temperature I should have done more justice to the magnificent
old glass of the windows—which glowed through the icy
dusk like the purple and orange of a winter sunset—
and to the immense sculptured external casing of the
choir. This latter is an extraordinary piece of work. It
is a high Gothic screen, shutting in the choir, and covered with elaborate bas-reliefs of the sixteenth and seventeenth centuries, representing scenes from the life of
Christ and of the Virgin. Some of the figures are admirable, and the effect of the whole great semicircular
wall, chiseled like a silver bowl, is superb. There is also
a crypt of high antiquity and, I believe, great interest,
to be seen; but my teeth chattered a respectful negative
to the sacristan who offered to guide me to it. It was so
agreeable to stand in the warm outer air again, that I
spent the rest of the day in it.

Although, besides its cathedral, Chartres has no very
rare architectural treasures, the place is picturesque,

in a shabby, third-rate, poverty-stricken sort of fashion, and my observations were not unremunerative. There is a little church of Saint Aignan, of the sixteenth century, with an elegant, decayed façade, and a small tower beside it, lower than its own roof, to which it is joined, in quaint, Siamese-twin fashion, by a single long buttress. Standing there with its crumbling Renaissance doorway in a kind of grass-grown alcove, it reminded me of what the tourist encounters in small Italian towns. Most of the streets of Chartres are crooked lanes, winding over the face of the steep hill, the summit of the hill being occupied by half-a-dozen little open squares, which seem like reservoirs of the dullness and stillness that flow through the town. In the midst of one of them rises an old dirty brick obelisk, commemorating the glories of the young General Marceau of the First Republic—"soldier at sixteen, general at twenty-three, he died at twenty-seven." [2] Chartres gives us an impression of extreme antiquity, but it is an antiquity that has gone down in the world. I saw very few of those stately little *hôtels*, with pilastered fronts, which look so well in the silent streets of provincial towns. The houses are mostly low, small, and of sordid aspect, and though many of them have overhanging upper stories, and steep, battered gables, there is nothing very exquisite in their quaintness.

I was struck, as an American always is in small French and English towns, with the immense number of shops, and their brilliant appearance, which seems so out of proportion to any visible body of consumers.

At Chartres the shopkeepers must all feed upon each other, for, whoever buys, the whole population sells. The population in the streets appears to consist of several hundred brown old peasant women, between seventy and eighty years of age, with their faces cross-hatched with wrinkles and their quaint white coifs drawn tightly over their weather-blasted eyebrows. Labor-stricken grandams, all the world over, are the reverse of lovely, for the toil that wrestles for its daily bread, morsel by morsel, is not beautifying; but I thought I had never seen the possibilities of female ugliness so variously embodied as in the crones of Chartres. Some of them were leading small children by the hand—little red-cheeked girls, in the close black caps and black pinafores of humble French infancy—a costume which makes French children always look like orphans. Those who feel very "strongly" on the subject of these little people being put out to nurse, as they generally are, may maintain that there is truth in the symbol. Others of the old women were guiding along the flinty lanes the steps of small donkeys, some of them fastened into little carts, others with well-laden backs. These were the only quadrupeds I perceived at Chartres. Neither horse nor carriage did I behold, save at the station the omnibuses of the rival inns—the Grand Monarque and the Duc de Chartres—which glare at each other across the Grande Place. A friend of mine told me that a few years ago, passing through Chartres, he went by night to call upon a gentleman who lived there. During his visit it came on to rain violently, and

when the hour for his departure arrived the rain had
made the streets impassable. There was no vehicle to be
had, and my friend was resigning himself to a soaking.
"You can be taken of course in the sedan chair," said
his host with dignity. The sedan chair was produced,
a couple of servingmen grasped the handles, my friend
stepped into it, and went swinging back—through the
last century—to the Grand Monarque. This little anecdote, I imagine, still paints Chartres socially.

Before dinner I took a walk on the planted promenade which encircles the town—the Tour-de-ville it is
called—much of which is extremely picturesque. Chartres has lost her walls as a whole, but here and there
they survive, and play a desultory part in holding the
town together. In one place the rampart is really magnificent—smooth, strong, and lofty, curtained with ivy,
and supporting on its summit an old convent and its
garden. Only one of the city gates remains—a narrow
arch of the fourteenth century, flanked by two admirable round towers, and preceded by a fosse. If you
stoop a little, as you stand outside, the arch of this
hoary old gate makes a most picturesque setting for
the picture of the interior of the town, and on the inner
hilltop against the sky the large gray mass of the Cathedral. The ditch is full, and to right and to left it
flows along the base of the moldering wall, through
which the shabby backs of houses extrude, and which
is garnished with little wooden galleries, lavatories of
the town's soiled linen. These little galleries are filled
with washerwomen, who crane over and dip their many-

colored rags into the yellow stream. The old patched and interrupted wall, the ditch with its weedy edges, the spots of color, the white-capped laundresses in their little wooden cages—one lingers to look at it all. To wind up the day I dined at the table d'hôte at the Grand Monarque, in a company of *voyageurs de commerce*, where I continued my observations. The dinner costs three francs fifty centimes; the landlord sits at the table and carves the meats, now and then manipulating a recalcitrant joint rather freely; the guests empty the dregs of their glasses on the floor, and clean their knives and forks, between the courses, with bread crumbs. But even among these circumstances the classic French art of conversation is by no means lost, and in paying my three francs fifty centimes I felt that I was paying for something more than my material dinner.

HENRY JAMES, JR.

April 29, 1876

13

PARISIAN FESTIVITY

Letter from Henry James, Jr.

REAPPEARANCE OF THE BRITISH TOURIST—THE CAR-
ROUSEL AT THE PALAIS DE L'INDUSTRIE—CYNICAL AR-
TISTS—M. MERMET'S OPERA OF "JEANNE D'ARC"—RE-
CENT BOOKS

[FROM A REGULAR CORRESPONDENT OF THE "TRIBUNE"]

———————◆———————

PARIS, April 22.—To say there has been nothing at
all to see, to hear, or to talk about during any given
fortnight in Paris is doubtless never a perfectly exact
statement; but I may safely say that for a couple of
weeks past the objects of interest have been rather of
the minor order. Holy Week has come and gone, and
the Easter holidays are now running their course. During the former brief period the spirit of profanity was
exercised much more effectually than I had supposed
possible in this epicurean city. For a week Paris was
palpably dull—it seemed like a scene at the play when
the gaslights have been lowered. The impression was increased by a sudden visitation of cold and sleet, and
Good Friday was really almost austere. People in search
of amusement needed sharp eyes to find it, and the wait-

ers at the restaurants were almost aggressive in their offers of fish. As regards Easter, what we are having is much more an English than a French holiday. Early on Monday morning the British tourist made his appearance on the boulevards, and he has been visible at every turn ever since. He has fairly taken possession of the city, and if his presence is fleeting it is, so to speak, intense. You recognize him farther off than you do an American; he makes a more vivid spot in the picture. He is always and everywhere the same—carrying with him, in his costume and physiognomy, that indefinable expression of not considering anything out of England worth making, physically or morally, a toilet for. The unanimity with which Englishmen abroad undress is indeed something surprising, and, say what we will, it seems to me in a certain way to be a sort of proof of that element of the still untamed and barbarous which some observers profess to find in the national character. I am sure M. Taine, for instance, never meets of an evening a flannel-shirted, pea-jacketed, soft-hatted son of Albion, followed by his robust feminine shadow, all blonde chignon and linsey-woolsey, without murmuring to himself that the "Vikings" and "Berserkers," the offspring of the north wind and the sea fog, are not extinct. Civilization has modified them, he must say, but it has not really altered them. No race carries a heavier external load of proprieties and conventional observances, but they are all on the surface, they have not been absorbed, and on the slightest pretext the natural man reasserts himself. A good pretext is found in a visit to this brilliant and exquisite Paris, the mother of arts and graces! What better proof of the undercurrent of barbarism in the British temperament can there be (we may still imagine the foreign critic inquiring) than the simple fact of the whole British nation going into dishabille in this aesthetically sacred spot? This has been a beautiful day, and I have had occasion to walk about much in the streets. Every few moments I have encountered an English family—papa, mamma, and daughters—gazing into a shopwindow, inquiring the way of the proprietress of a newspaper kiosk, or climbing into or out of a cab. I came home with a lively reflection uppermost in my mind—what a godsend is the British tourist to the French caricaturist! The French are an ugly race, if you will; the national type lacks dignity. The English are a handsome race; they have nobler lines and a grander mold than their neighbors; and yet, given the British physiognomy as you see it, at the end of protruded necks, on the boulevards and the Rue de Rivoli, and given the subtle, the acute, the diabolical French perception of external facts, and it is not hard to decide in whose shoes, for the moment, we would rather stand. My own fingers, as I walked along, itched for the pencil of "Cham" or of Daumier.[1]

This is not only the time of the English, it is also the time of the exhibitions. There have been two or three already at the Palais de l'Industrie, and the series is to culminate in ten days, in the opening of the Salon of 1876. The last was the great annual horse fair—an entertainment known here by the more elegant designation of a "Concours Hippique." It lasted a fortnight, but I shall not attempt to recite its glories, being a stranger to the mysteries of horse flesh. I was present the last day, however, at a spectacle which it took no particular initiation to enjoy. The Concours terminates every year in what is here called a Carrousel—a display of purely fantastic and picturesque horsemanship. The Carrousel was held this year by the cadets of the cavalry school of Saumur, and was in every way a high festival. The whole vast nave of the Palais de l'Industrie was converted into an oblong arena, and though the price of admission had been made high, to exclude the populace, the crowd was mighty. Apart from it, under a dais, sat the President of the Republic and Mme. MacMahon, like a medieval king and queen presiding at a tournament. It was simply the circus idealized— or rather, more correctly, realized. The knights and cavaliers who rode at the Saracens' heads and hurled their lances (this last not very felicitously, by the way) at the great mask of the blackamoor, were real young knights, with trappings not of tinsel, and holding their honor and their lives in their hands. It was all very graceful and gorgeous and effective—for those amiable minds at least that linger over the picturesque wherever they find it, and are ashamed to ask it impertinent questions. Such minds, at such a spectacle, may here and there have found themselves excusable for reflecting on the exclusively brilliant side of military pretensions. Standing armies are abominable things, the necessity of maintaining upward of a million of men for pure destruction is an insupportable burden to a country, and the armed suspense in which all Europe is living is a reproach to civilization—all that is most uncontestable. And yet—horrible as the statement may sound—the contemplative American often finds himself wishing, or half wishing, that his native land had, as a regular thing, some knowledge of the military incubus. Don't call him too rudely to account—his reasons are purely sentimental; he is willing to admit even that they are immoral. He can only say, in his irresponsible depravity, that living in a country where the army is a great fact has opened his perceptions to some of the good effects of having the military virtues and the military spectacle constantly before one's eyes. They are an expensive luxury, certainly; but it is proper after all to pay high for the maintenance, in an honorable style, of such qualities as gallantry and bravery. The French, in spite of their humiliation and defeats, are to my sense extremely fond of their army; they love it, they enjoy it, and admire it; they watch it and judge it with a kind of romantic tenderness. I felt this the other day at the Carrousel in question; there was a sort of arrested murmur of affection and delight running constantly through the vast assembly. *"Ah, qu'il est gentil, ce petit Saumurien!"* you heard your neighbors exclaim; and there was a loving cadence in the phrase that made me envy the sentiment that produced it. I envied the state of mind from which it sprung, as a part of the regular daily consciousness of the citizen—and I envied the country the possession of the brightly habited class which was the object of it. This audacious apology for an argument amounts, perhaps after all, to the statement that hair-splitters may discern, if they choose to take the trouble, that in being without a standing army a country loses a few good things, as well as a vast number of bad ones.

An exhibition for which I may at least claim that it can give rise (at any rate in my own mind) to no dangerous perversities of taste is that of the little group of the Irreconcilables—otherwise known as the "Impressionists" in painting.[2] It is being held during the present month at Durand-Ruel's, and I have found it decidedly interesting. But the effect of it was to make me think better than ever of all the good old rules which decree that beauty is beauty and ugliness ugliness, and warn us off from the sophistications of satiety. The young contributors to the exhibition of which I speak are partisans of unadorned reality and absolute foes to arrangement, embellishment, selection, to the artist's allowing himself, as he has hitherto, since art began, found his best account in doing, to be preoccupied with the idea of the beautiful. The beautiful, to them, is what the supernatural is to the Positivists—a metaphysical notion, which can only get one into a muddle and is to be severely let alone. Let it alone, they say, and it will come at its own pleasure; the painter's proper field is simply the actual, and to give a vivid impression of how a thing happens to look, at a particular moment, is the essence of his mission. This attitude has something in common with that of the English Preraphaelites, twenty years ago, but this little band is on all grounds less interesting than the group out of which Millais and Holman Hunt rose into fame. None of its members show signs of possessing first-rate talent, and indeed the "Impressionist" doctrines strike me as incompatible, in an artist's mind, with the existence of first-rate talent. To embrace them you must be provided with a plentiful absence of imagination. But the divergence in method between the English Preraphaelites and this little group is especially striking, and very characteristic of the moral differences of the French and English races. When the English realists "went in," as the phrase is, for hard truth and stern fact, an irresistible instinct of righteousness caused them to try to purchase forgiveness for their infidelity to the old more or less moral proprieties and conventionalities, by an exquisite, patient, virtuous manipulation—by being above all things laborious. But the Impressionists, who, I think, are more consistent, abjure virtue altogether, and declare that a subject which has been crudely chosen shall be loosely treated. They send detail to the dogs and concentrate themselves on general expression. Some of their generalizations of expression are in a high degree curious. The Englishmen, in a word, were pedants, and the Frenchmen are cynics.

Among the exhibitions, I take it, may be ranked M. Mermet's new opera, *Jeanne d'Arc*,[3] which, after being kept back for many years and a great deal talked about, has at last been produced. It was in rehearsal at the time of the destruction by fire of the old Opera house, and the composer's score was one of the very few objects snatched from the flames. Thus providentially rescued, it would seem that M. Mermet's work had been reserved for a brilliant destiny. It has found one to a certain extent in being put upon the stage at the new Opera with extraordinary splendor, and rendered by Faure and Mlle. Krauss with exemplary zeal; but here its good fortune stops. It has made no advance in the public favor; it is pronounced hopelessly dull and tame. Even to an auditor to whom musical things are fathomless mysteries, and who, if he fails to appreciate good music, finds in general a compensation in not suffering from bad, the ponderosity of *Jeanne d'Arc* seemed the other night sufficiently palpable. There is only one voice to proclaim it, and M. Mermet must wish his work had been left to the charity of the flames —they would have been kinder than the critics. The opera is played to full houses, however, thanks to the splendor of the spectacle and to the affluence of strangers who desire to see the house on any terms. The *mise en scène* is indeed superb, and more perfect than anything of the same sort that I have ever seen. There is in particular a certain representation of the gardens of the castle of Blois, with the long mass of the château foreshortened in the sunshine above them, and the goodly Loire country receding in the distance beyond the winding, shining rivers, and beneath a vast, bright summer sky, which reaches the highest ideal of scene painting. There is also a ballet of *ribaudes*—camp maidens and female vagabonds—which is the perfection of the expensive picturesque.

I have on my table three or four books of which I had meant to speak, but I have as usual left myself little space for literature. The literary remains of Sainte-Beuve [4] are being brought to light with merciless energy—the *Chroniques Parisiennes* and the *Cahiers de Sainte-Beuve* having appeared within two or three weeks of each other. I use the word "merciless" rather with regard to the great critic's victims than to his own reputation. The emptying of table drawers of memoranda after an eminent writer's death has always a disagreeable and painful side, [5] but if this posthumous rummaging is ever justifiable, it may pass in the case of Sainte-Beuve. His literary house was always in such good order that an irregular visit will discover no untidiness, and moreover he belonged to that only small order of minds for which it may be claimed that their lightest thoughts and utterances have a value. But some of his friends and acquaintances will be more interested than gratified to read the notes and observations he made upon their conversation and talents for his own use. He was sharp enough in his *causeries* with the public, but he was sharper still in tête-à-tête with himself. It is interesting to have a glimpse of his literary practices—to see how he lived pen in hand and took notes not only upon what he read but upon what he heard, thought, felt, and dreamed. Never was there so literary a life. Another book of the hour is Émile Zola's [6] new novel, *Son Excellence Eugène Rougon,* which has attained a success not hitherto enjoyed by the productions of this remarkable young writer. The success of the present work is owing partly to its cleverness, partly to the fact that it is a presentation, through a transparent veil, of actual persons, and chiefly, I suspect, to its brutal indecency. Eugène Rougon is Eugène Rouher, M. de Marsy is M. de Morny, and the initiated will tell you who Clorinda Balbi, the heroine, is. This last is a most amazing portrait. Émile Zola, a "pupil" of Gustave Flaubert, is, as a novelist, the most thoroughgoing of the little band of the out-and-out realists. Unfortunately the real, for him, means exclusively the unclean, and he utters his crudities with an air of bravado which makes them doubly intolerable.

HENRY JAMES, JR.

May 13, 1876

14

ART IN FRANCE

Letter from Henry James, Jr.

THE SALON OF 1876—GREATNESS OF THE DISPLAY—
DORÉ'S COLOSSAL CANVAS—LARGE PAINTINGS BY MON-
CHABLON, BIN, AND BLANC——M. SYLVESTRE'S PORTRAYAL
OF NERO—EXCELLENCE OF M. DETAILLE'S WAR SCENE

[FROM A REGULAR CORRESPONDENT OF THE "TRIBUNE"]

PARIS, May 5.—I find no difficulty today in deciding
what to write about; for chroniclers and talkers there
is only one possible subject. The Salon—the ninety-
third in the history of the institution—opened a few
days since, and all the scribblers are mending their
pens.[1] I have paid three visits to the Palais de l'Industrie (in which the exhibition is held), and I have, I believe—from my own point of view—separated the sheep
from the goats, and earned the right to attempt some
coherent discourse. It seems at first as if coherency in
one's impressions would be slow to arrive; the first effect of so vast an array of pictures, pervaded by a
high average of cleverness, is most bewildering and confounding. The Salon this year is very large; there are,
exclusive of drawings and cartoons and without mak-

ing mention of sculpture, 2,095 pictures. The regulation enacted during the present year, in virtue of which an artist has a right to exhibit but two works, has not had the effect of reducing the exhibition numerically; it contains upward of a hundred pictures more than that of 1875. It is, moreover, not of exceptional brilliancy; the number of works which make landmarks in its long-drawn extent is not large. It is hardly more than a fair average salon—though it must be added that it may be only this and yet leave a lively impression of cleverness upon the Anglo-Saxon visitors.

Amid such a chaos of productions it is hard to know how to measure conflicting claims or what to speak of first. The easiest course is perhaps to let simple size take precedence, and to dismiss at once what are called the "machines" of the exhibition. Large pictures in France are usually spoken of as *de la peinture de style;* a properly constituted salon must have a certain number of them; they are a sort of propitiatory offering to the "high-toned" Muse. This year there are a great many such offerings, but in each of these quality and quantity are to my sense more than ever divorced. For simple brute size a colossal canvas by Gustave Doré carries off the palm—a canvas presenting to us M. Doré's conception of "Christ's Entrance into Jerusalem." I do not see what old memories of admiration for Gustave Doré's genius in the days when he treated it with common humanity should avail to make an even very amiable critic hesitate to speak of this as a rather shameless performance. M. Doré treats his genius now

as you wouldn't treat a tough and patient old cab
horse; I know of few spectacles more painful in the
annals of art. Imagine a colored print from the supple-
ment of an illustrated paper magnified a thousandfold
and made to cover almost a whole side of a great hall,
and you have M. Doré's sacred picture. A vast, garish
crowd is sprawling on its knees over a mass of palm
boughs, in front of a pasteboard colonnade, through
one of the arches of which a figure which a school boy
might have daubed advances on an ass. There is no
color—or worse than none—no drawing, no expression,
no feeling, no remotest hint of detail; nothing but an
immense mechanical facility, from which every vestige
of charm and imagination has departed. But it is really
very *naïf* on my part to be so explicit. There is an immense Jeanne d'Arc by M. Monchablon, bounding over
agglomerated corpses, brandishing her sword and hero-
ically screaming; I don't know what sustained the artist
through the execution of this very spacious work—it
was not the force of talent. There is a great canvas
representing "Harmony," for a governmental ceiling,
by M. Bin, full of elegant muses and foreshortened lute
players; (M. Bin's picture, which is meant to be above
one's head, horizontally, is hung against the wall, and
the spectator in consequence is made to feel as if he,
tipsily, had lost his proper standpoint—an imputation
which he resents by not admiring the picture as much,
perhaps, as he ought to do). There is a brilliant and
elegant group from Ariosto by M. Joseph Blanc—the
deliverance of Angelica from the sea monster—the most

agreeable, to my mind, of the big pictures. It is a kind
of picture which leaves us cold, but it is very good of
its kind—painted in a high, light tone, full of pinks
and light blues and other elegant tints, but with a
great deal of skill of arrangement and refinement of
taste. It is the only one of the *tableaux de style* which
seems to me to possess much style. Style is what M.
Laccetti, who paints in quite a different tone, and
affects intense browns and powerful shadows, has aimed
at in his "Orestes and the Furies." He has only half
hit it, I think, but he has missed it with a good deal
of vigor and picturesqueness.

The striking picture of the year and the one, probably, to which nineteen twentieths of the visitors to the
salon attribute most talent, is a great subject by M.
Sylvestre—a "Locusta trying the effects of poisons
before Nero." As a subject the thing is detestable, inasmuch as it allows almost no chance for beauty; but as
an accomplished and picturesque piece of painting of
the younger, larger, and richer academic sort, com-
bining a good deal of reality with a good deal of arrangement, it is a remarkable success. I suppose the
picture is marked for the medal of honor—or at least
for the first medal in painting. Nero is seated, leaning
forward, with his elbow on the back of his chair, and
his hand over his mouth, watching the contortions of
a slave who, extended on the pavement, is expiring in
agony before him. Beside him, and nearer the spectator,
is seated the horrible Locusta, descanting upon the
properties of her dose, her face turned toward him and

her arm, with a strangely familiar gesture, lying across
his knee—the movement of the outstretched hand
meanwhile giving point to her explanation. She is a
gaunt, swarthy gypsy, half naked, and with the profile
of a murderess. Nero is both listening and watching,
and the grave, intent, inquisitive depravity of his dark,
fat, youthful face is very cleverly rendered. The portentous familiarity, the sinister "chattiness" of this
precious couple is indeed in a high degree effective.
But the strong point of the picture is the figure of
the victim of their interesting experiment—the slave
who is writhing in a horrible spasm upon the polished
marble pavement. This is strong drawing and strong
painting, and it does great honor to the young artist.
The man is a magnificent fellow, in his prime, with a
fair beard and a yellow headcloth, and he stretches out
his arms with an agonized movement which is at once
very real and very noble. Into this figure, indeed, the
painter has introduced a certain element of beauty—it
has great breadth and yet much detail, great solidity
and yet not a little elegance. It is, in a word, very intelligent. But there is something vulgar in the way the
picture is lighted, something coarse in its tone, something in the effect it produces that falls below the talent
that has been expended upon it. M. Sylvestre is not a
painter who sets you dreaming about his future. The
same subject has been treated by another artist, M.
Aublet, with inferior although with noticeable skill.
M. Aublet gives us three or four poisoned slaves, wrig-
gling over the pavement in different attitudes; the

effect is slightly grotesque—they suggest toads hopping out after a shower. This simple jest is not heartless, inasmuch as M. Aublet's slaves do not produce a lively impression of reality. His picture is flanked on each side by an equally huge and much less clever scene of torture—one, a so-called "Diversion of a Courtesan" —a lady reclining on a gigantic couch and watching a slave bleed to death at her feet (I recommend the subject), the other "Clytemnestra and Agamemnon," reeking with blood and mediocrity. It is a charming trio, and it is a great pity it should not be seen by those critics in Berlin who affirm that French art is chiefly remarkable for its cruelty.

If M. Sylvestre's picture is the most impressive in the Salon, I have no doubt that the most popular will be the contribution of M. Detaille, the admirable military painter. It is indeed already, of all the pictures, the most closely surrounded, and it has a good right to its honors. It is called "En Reconnaissance," and represents a battalion of chasseurs coming into a village street in which a cavalry fight has just taken place and scattered its trophies over the ground. A squad of sharpshooters is preceding the rest of the troop and advancing cautiously along the crooked, bloodstained lane. They have paused and are scanning the lay of the land in front of them—the leader checking them with a backward movement of his hand, while he listens to an urchin who has come up to speak to him—a patriot of thirteen, in blouse and muffler, doing his boyish best to be useful, and give damaging information. This boy, with his light, small body, so well indicated beneath his thin blouse, his cold red face, his hand in his pocket, his scanty trousers, is the great success of the picture; in the gesture with which he points, eagerly and modestly, down the street there is something singularly vivid and true. On the right, in the foreground, a Prussian lancer and his horse have lately tumbled head foremost; though they are not yet cold they are pitifully and awkwardly dead. A couple of the sharpshooters are glancing down at them as they pass, with different expressions—"It served him right" in one case; "It's a bad business at best" in the other. These men are all admirably studied. On the left a gendarme, badly wounded, has collapsed against a garden wall, through the open gate of which a man, peeping out, is trying to drag him in. In the rear, through the gray snowy air, the rest of the chasseurs are coming up. The picture is remarkably perfect and complete—a page torn straight from unpublished history. The variety and vividness of the types, the expressiveness of the scene, without a touch of exaggeration or grimace, the dismal chill of the weather, the sense of possible bullets in the air, the full man size of the little figures, the clean, consummate brilliancy of the painting, make it a work of which nothing but good is to be said.

The picture which will appeal most strongly to the inner circle of observers—those who enjoy a first-class method more than an entertaining story—is unquestionably the much-noticed, the already famous "Intérieur d'Atelier" of M. Munkacsy. It divides with

one other work, to my sense, the claim of being the
most masterly piece of painting in the Salon. The other
work is a portrait, of which I will presently speak.
Meanwhile M. Munkacsy, who is a Hungarian, with
a Parisian reputation already established, comes so
near the absolute of solid and superb painting that it
little matters how we settle the question of pre-emi-
nence. I do not know when I have seen a piece of artistic
work of any kind which struck me as having so purely
masculine a quality. M. Munkacsy's painting is strong
as a rich baritone voice is strong—in the same personal
and closely characteristic way. Imagine the baritone
voice admirably educated and master of every secret
and mystery of vocalism, and the analogy is complete.
M. Munkacsy belongs to the school of painters for
whom a "subject" is simply any handsome object what-
soever—anything materially paintable. He does not
resort to history or mythology for his themes, and it
doubtless seems as absurd to him that you should have
to look at a picture with one eye on a literary paragraph in a catalogue, as that you should listen to a
song with one ear applied to a tube into which a spoken
explanation should be injected. His subject here is
simply a handsome woman in a blue velvet dress sitting in profile before an easel on which stands a small
landscape, and of a man (the painter himself) lounging against a table between her and the easel. The lady
is bent forward, her hands are pressed together in her
lap, she is looking intently and appreciatively before
her; the artist, who is in light drab garments, presents

his full face, but turns it slightly askance, and eyes his work more critically. There is nothing here very new and strange, and yet the picture is admirably full and rich. It is composed in what I believe painters call an extremely low key—it is an extraordinary harmony of the deepest tones, unrelieved by a touch of light color or by more than a gleam of high light. And yet in spite of the sort of unctuous brown cavern of which the studio seems at first to consist, you presently perceive that there is nothing cheap or brutal in the artist's dusky accumulations of color, that everything is defined, harmonized, and made to play a part. The painting has incomparable breadth and freedom, and yet all its rich, bold brush work has been admirably wrought, and, as it were, melted together. There are almost no sensible lines anywhere, and yet there is no sensible evasion of line; it is rare to see a picture in which draughtmanship is so enveloped and muffled in color. There is plenty of detail, and yet it is all detail in such warm, fluid juxtaposition that you are conscious of it only through your general impression of richness. The heads are admirable—full of solidity and relief; the only complaint to be made of them is that they are painted too much in the same tone and on the same level as the inanimate parts of the picture. A little more rosiness, a little infusion of light, would not have spoiled them. The blue velvet dress of the lady is, however, the great triumph. It is one of the most interesting pieces of frippery that I have seen in many a day, and the way it is painted is a sort of résumé of the manner of the whole picture. It is the work of a man who stands completely outside of it and its superficial appeals, and has, regarding its texture and tone, a vision, a judgment, and a conviction of his own. This second solution, as the apothecaries say, of blue velvet a trifle faded and worn, has a peculiar charm. I meant to add a word about the magnificent portrait of M. Wallon, the late Minister of Public Instruction, by M. Bastien-Lepage—the gem, to my mind, of the exhibition. But I shall be obliged, with your permission, to devote another letter to the Salon, and I defer my remarks. I shall not be sorry, on the ground of not having yet committed myself to utterance about it, to go and look at the picture again.

HENRY JAMES, JR.

May 27, 1876

15

ART IN PARIS

Letter from Henry James, Jr.

THE SALON REVISITED——DISTINCTIVE MERITS OF THE
PRINCIPAL PORTRAITS——PAINTINGS BY MM. GÉRÔME,
CABANEL, BOUGUEREAU, AND VIBERT——M. MOREAU'S
ARTISTIC VAGARIES——THE LANDSCAPES AND THE STATU-
ARY

[FROM A REGULAR CORRESPONDENT OF THE "TRIBUNE"]

PARIS, May 6.—In my last letter I gave but an incomplete account of the Salon. I was obliged to leave
some of the most interesting works unmentioned.[1]
Among these is the portrait of M. Wallon, the late
Minister of Public Instruction, by M. Bastien-Lepage,
certainly the best portrait in the exhibition, and in a
certain sense the most perfect work. It is rather dry
and literal, it lacks freedom and style, but it is a masterly piece of painting, and it possesses, if not a high,
at least a very solid interest. It represents an old man
of a sedentary, scholarly complexion, with a bald, re-
treating forehead—the forehead retreats admirably—
a pair of clear, pale blue eyes, and a face puckered
and kneaded and softly bruised, as it were, by Time.

The modeling of the face, the minute detail of the complexion, the distinct yet subdued relief of the nose, the vaguely chafed and frost-nipped tones about the mouth—all this is admirable. It is patient, analytic, unimaginative painting, but the result is a remarkable expression of reality—a reality which, in the face, vividly recalls Holbein. Holbein, however, would have given his subject a better body than M. Bastien-Lepage has done. There are no ribs or limbs beneath the black coat and trousers which indicate the figure, the painter's skill in modeling seeming to have exhausted itself in the face. It revives, indeed, briefly in the hands, which are placed flatly, with strictly historic awkwardness, on each of the knees, and are admirable in their mottled, elderly plumpness. On the whole, it is a very fine portrait in a secondary manner—which I think is better than being a second-rate work in a grand manner. If the merit of a work of art is to be measured by the completeness with which it executes what it attempts, this performance of M. Bastien-Lepage deserves a very honorable mention. I may as well speak at once of the other portraits—or of such of them as are worth being commemorated. The number, of course, is enormous, and the cumulative effects of so many expansive effigies, in elaborated toilets, or in still more elaborate dishabille, each addressing its own peculiar simper to the promiscuous throng that tramps through the exhibition, is no less irritating than usual. The level of clearness, so high in all French painting, strikes me as rather lower in the line of portraiture

than elsewhere; nevertheless there is plenty of the
cleverness to which it is not necessary to allude. M.
Carolus-Duran, the fashionable portrait painter *par
excellence*, represents M. Émile de Girardin composing
an editorial at a writing table, and a lady in a white
ball dress coming downstairs, with her hand on the
balustrade. Both pictures are below his reputation. M.
de Girardin's pale face appears to have been "enam-
eled" for the occasion; it is suffused with a vulgar and
unnatural bloom. His hands, which are apparently
handsome (after the plump French model), are, however, rather skillfully painted. The lady on the stairs
is a decided failure; her bare arm, following the line
of the balustrade, takes two or three twists and turns
too many, and her satin-shod foot, seeking the lower
step, gropes downward like that of a blind person. Add
to this that the lady is holding up her head with an
air which seems to proclaim that if there are two things
in which, more than in others, she takes a pardonable
satisfaction, they are her arm and her foot. There is
a charming portrait by M. Baudry of a tall, slim, de-
lightfully lady-like person, seated and looking at the
world over the back of a gilded chair; and there is a
representation by M. Cabanel of a young lady of great
natural advantages—snowy arms and shoulders, and
vividly auburn tresses—standing very bravely up to
display them.

There are pink-fingered *chiffonné* young women by
Chaplin, whom one can scarcely approach for their
admirers, and who look as if they had been painted

with a compound of distilled rose leaves and dewdrops.
It is a very light painting, certainly; but a great deal
of talent has gone to making it light. The talent, however, had better have gone elsewhere. There are two
agreeable, and for a woman sufficiently solid, portraits
by Mlle. Jacquemart, who sprang into fame a few years
since with a remarkable portrait of M. Thiers. But her
present work would not have made her famous, and
will hardly even keep her so. She had the misfortune
to make a hit, and she is now paying, in relative ob-
scurity, the penalty. One of the most interesting portraits in the Salon is that of the great Russian novelist,
Tourguéneff, by a young Russian artist of high promise, M. Harlamoff, who attracted notice last year by
a remarkable portrait of Mme. Pauline Viardot. Half
the interest of M. Harlamoff's picture, this year as
well, is in the admirable physiognomy of the model,
which would have offered a sovereign resistance to trivial treatment; but it is also a very robust and brilliantly simple piece of painting. M. Tourguéneff, clad
in a brown velvet coat, sits with his hands in his lap,
presenting his full face, which is pervaded by an air
of intense and sinister revery. This expression is powerfully rendered, but it has the great fault of not being
that of the least irritable of men of genius. A work
which has at the least its share of gazers is a huge representation, by M. Clairin, of Mlle. Sarah Bernhardt,
the bright particular star of the Comédie Française.
Considering the very small space which this young
lady takes up in nature—her thinness is quite phe-

nomenal—she occupies a very large one at the Salon. M. Clairin's portrait is vast and superficially brilliant, but really, I think, not above mediocrity. There is a remarkable white satin wrapper, in which the actress, who is lolling on a sort of oriental divan, is twisted and entangled with something of her peculiar snake-like grace, and which shines from afar; and there are draperies and plants and rugs, and a great deerhound. The only thing wanting is Mlle. Bernhardt herself. She is wanting even more in her second portrait, by Mlle. Louise Abbéma, in which she is standing, in a black walking dress; and in this almost equally large work there are no accessories, good or bad, to make up for the deficiency.

M. Bonnat, whose superb portrait of Mme. Pasca in the last Salon was the picture of the year, has added nothing to his reputation by his present performance —a large "Jacob wrestling with the Angel." Two naked athletes, in a sort of flesh-colored cave, are interlocking their arms and legs and clinching their teeth; but neither of them is moving an inch—which indeed is quite natural, as they are composed, to all appearance, of rose-colored granite. The picture contains some very vigorous drawing, but little painting and no interest. It is a powerful but almost unredeemed failure. If M. Bonnat, from whom much was expected, has given two poor figures, M. Vollon, from whom nothing was expected, has produced a magnificent one. M. Vollon has been hitherto an admired painter of landscape and *natures mortes*, but until this year he had not given

his full measure. His "Fishwife of Dieppe" is one of
the finest things in the Salon, and all the finer for
having a certain generous amateurishness of manner.
One sees that M. Vollon's figure is half experimental;
but this only augments the pleasure of seeing it so successful. A tall, bare-legged peasant woman, in a dusky
white cap, a tattered kilt, and a chemise so ragged that
it exposes completely her strong brown shoulders and
bosom, is moving across the shore with long steps and
with an empty fishing basket hung on her back. The
picture is hardly more than a sketch; it has no brilliancy of color, and the background is a mere indication; but the character of the picture is at once so true
and so noble, the action is so free, the poise of the head,
the swing of the legs, the lightness of the step are so
happily seized, and yet in so just and delicate a measure idealized, that the whole expression is strikingly
grand. The body is admirably painted; the legs are
animated human limbs. M. Vollon, after this, I suppose, will not hide his light under a bushel. Among the
French painters best known in America, M. Gérôme is,
as usual, conspicuous for his cleverness. He exhibits a
small picture of a "Santon at the door of a Mosque"—
a characteristically hard and brilliant piece of oriental-
ism. A great square-shouldered dervish, with his filthy
body all but entirely naked, his head shaved, and his
huge mouth contorted with pious vociferation, is apparently keeping guard over a congregation of shoes
which the ingoing worshipers have deposited on the
threshold of a Mussulman temple. It was for these

shoes, I suspect, that the picture was painted, and as they are treated they are quite worth it. They are of all sizes, colors, and shapes, and full of ingenious expression. They make a very picturesque, an almost dramatic array. M. Cabanel's second picture is the property, I see by the catalogue, of a lady of New York. It represents the spouse of the Song of Solomon, sitting cross-legged on the ground and gazing upward, in a mystical languor of love, divine or profane, as one may choose. She is a very handsome Jewess; her eyes are long, her flesh transparent, and her draperies very elegant. Apropos of transparent flesh, the inexhaustible M. Bouguereau exhibits two pictures characterized by all his extraordinary skill and his abuse of tones and glossy surfaces. It is a standing wonder that a man can paint at once so finely and so perversely. The larger of M. Bouguereau's pictures, a *Piété* of many figures, contains passages of drawing and even of painting which many an artist would be glad to sign with his name who would yet be quite ashamed to stand responsible for the thin, manufactured interest and the china-plate aspect of the whole. A few years ago M. Gustave Moreau made a series of brilliant appearances at the Salon as the apostle of a new and strange treatment of mythological subjects. His mythology and his strangeness remain, but his novelty and his renown have somewhat waned. He is ingenious, erudite, and highly imaginative; if M. Gustave Flaubert, the eminent novelist, when he wrote his *Temptation of St. Anthony*, had been disposed to painting instead of writing, he would prob-

ably have gone to work in M. Moreau's fashion. M.
Moreau, with his "Hercules and the Hydra of Lernos"
and his "Salomé," has produced two very rare and curious works; he is an original and interesting, if not a
satisfactory colorist. But his performances enter completely, to my sense, into the domain of the arbitrary
and the fantastic, and I give up the attempt to follow
him. Too much of the arbitrary in a picture is as uncomfortable as a little is indispensable. A painter who
is greatly relished in America, where many of his pictures are owned, M. George Vibert, has two works, one
of which I should have mentioned among the portraits.
It represents, in emulation of M. Carolus-Duran, a
lady descending a staircase—but in a strictly possible
position; her hands crossed in front of her, and her
blue velvet dress and the train of her dress lying splen-
didly up the steps behind her. It is very rich and agreeable. M. Vibert's second work deals with a theme of
which he has made a specialty—the carnal infirmities,
humorously viewed, of monks and priests. In "L'Anti-
chambre de Monseigneur," a rubicund friar, waiting
for an audience with the Bishop, is making himself
agreeable to a pretty young country woman who is
seated beside him on a satin sofa, while another friar,
ostensibly reading his breviary, peeps round the corner
of a recess, over his shoulder, to see what his companion
is, in vulgar phrase, "up to." It is very clever storytell-
ing and very pretty painting. I have said nothing of
the landscapists, but it is not because they are not

numerous. I am exhausting my space. Besides, landscapes suffer at crowded exhibitions more than figure pieces; their want of isolation is more fatal to them, and a great effort is required to judge them as they are meant to be judged—on the artist's easel or the owner's favoring wall. Daubigny has two large performances which, although vigorous and expressive, have rather less even than usual of this powerful sketcher's moderate amount of charm. M. Daubigny is rather brutal. Not so M. Français—not enough so perhaps. There is always a touch of the historic, academic, arranged landscape in M. Français' pictures, but there is plenty of genuine nature too, and the combination is often admirable. This is the case this year. In the way of landscape the things I have most enjoyed are two low, long pictures by an admirable Polish artist—M. Chelmonski by name; a couple of winter scenes in Russia. One of them, the "Thaw in Ukraine," is a thorough masterpiece. A rickety sleigh has stopped at a village ale house, and its four horses, harnessed abreast, are steaming, fetlock deep, in the yellow slush of the highway. At the door are gathered a dozen figures, admirably real and admirably Russian; the inimitable *samovar*—the national tea urn—is deposited in the midst of them, in the filthy snow. The truth and vigor of this little scene are masterly—the black, panting, sweating horses, the rising dampness, the snow-charged sky, the high-thatched, smoke-swept roof of the hut, the extreme variety and vivacity of the figures. M. Chelmonski, if I am not mistaken, has been an admiring observer of that most delightful of Dutch painters, Salomon Ruysdael. I must add briefly that a number of American artists are represented at the Salon—among them being Messrs. May, Bacon, Edgar Ward, and Bridgman. Most of the contributions of these gentlemen are agreeable and entertaining—the most noticeable, perhaps, being Mr. Bacon's "Franklin at Home at Philadelphia."

The ground floor at the Palais de l'Industrie is converted by the Salon into a garden, reasonably blooming under the circumstances, and dotted with the contributions of sculpture. As usual, these are numerous, but everything this year is cast into the shade by the two figures of M. Paul Dubois—portions of a monument about to be erected to Gen. Lamoricière at Nantes. These two figures are of surpassing beauty, and altogether the most eminent works in the Salon. (M. Dubois is generally known by his charming "Florentine Singer," in bronze, now in the Museum of the Luxembourg.) I have left myself no space to speak of these images of "Charity" and "Military Courage"; I must content myself with recording briefly but emphatically my admiration for them. They are not only better in degree than any other work of art of the year; they are quite unique in kind. They are interesting and touched strongly with ideal beauty; they do the artist the greatest honor. Not to be utterly incomplete I must say that Mlle. Sarah Bernhardt, the actress, has a huge group of an old peasant woman holding in her lap, in a frenzied posture, the body of her drowned grandson. The thing is extremely amateurish, but it is surprisingly good for a young lady whom the public knows to draw upon her artistic ingenuity for so many other purposes.

HENRY JAMES, JR.

June 5, 1876

16

PARISIAN TOPICS

Letter from Henry James, Jr.

M. ERNEST RENAN'S NEW VOLUME—M. MICHELET'S FU-
NERAL—POLITICAL DISPLAY AVOIDED—MME. PLESSY'S
RETIREMENT FROM THE STAGE—A MINOR ART EXHIBI-
TION—PLANS FOR THE GREAT EXPOSITION OF 1878

[FROM A REGULAR CORRESPONDENT OF THE "TRIBUNE"]

PARIS, May 27.—M. Ernest Renan has just published a new volume,[1] which will not fail to find its way
speedily into the hands of all lovers of good writing.
A new volume by Renan is an intellectual feast; if he
is not the first of French writers, I don't know who
may claim the title. In these *Dialogues et Fragments
Philosophiques*, indeed, it is the dialogues alone that
are new; they occupy but half of the volume, the rest
of which is composed of reprinted pieces. The dialogues
are a sort of *jeu d'esprit*, but a *jeu d'esprit* of a very
superior kind—the recreation of a man of elevated
genius. They are prefaced by a few pages breathing a
very devoted patriotism, and proving that the author's
exorbitant intellectual reveries have not relaxed his
sense of the plain duties of citizenship. To win back

that esteem which he appears willing to concede that they have in some degree forfeited, he exhorts his fellow countrymen above all things to work. Let each, he says, surpass himself in his own particular profession, "so that the world may still cry of us, 'These Frenchmen are still the sons of their fathers; eighty years ago Condorcet, in the midst of the Reign of Terror, waiting for death in his hiding place in the Rue Servandoni, wrote his *Sketch of the Progress of the Human Mind.*' " M. Renan imagines a group of friends, who assemble in a quiet corner of a park of Versailles, to exchange reflections upon the "ensemble de l'Univers." The subject is extensive, and it may well take half a dozen talkers to cover the ground. Three persons, however, take the lead, each one of whom unfolds his particular view of the cosmos. These three views are classed by M. Renan under the respective heads of "Certainties," "Probabilities," and "Reveries." He disclaims them all as a representation of his own opinions, and says that he has simply entertained himself with imagining what might be urged and argued in each direction. It is probable, however, that if his convictions and feelings are not identical with those of either of his interlocutors, they have a great deal in common with the whole mass of the discussion, and that Philalethes, Theophrastus, and Theoctistes are but names for certain moods of M. Renan's mind. If so, one can only congratulate him upon the extraordinary ingenuity and fertility of his intellect and the entertaining company of his thoughts. These pages are full of good things admirably said, of brilliant and exquisite suggestions, and of happy contributions to human wisdom. Their fault is the fault which for some time has been increasing in M. Renan's writing—a sort of intellectual foppishness, a love of paradox and of distinction for distinction's sake. His great merit has always been his natural distinction, but now, in this same distinction, in the affectation of views which are nothing if not exquisite, views sifted and filtered through an infinite intellectual experience, there is something rather self-conscious and artificial. The reader cannot help wishing that M. Renan might be brought into more immediate contact with general life itself—general life as distinguished from that horizon of pure learning which surrounds the *cabinet de travail* of a Parisian scholar—suspecting that, if this could happen, some of his fine-spun doubts and perplexities would find a very natural solution, and some of his fallacies die a very natural death.

Philalethes, the exponent of M. Renan's "Certainties," is not so certain about some things as his friends might have expected; but his skepticism is narrowed down to a point just fine enough to be graceful. "In fact," he says, "if I had been a priest, I should never have been willing to accept a fee for my mass; I should have been afraid of doing as the shopkeeper who delivers for money an empty bag. Just so I should have had a scruple about drawing a profit from my religious beliefs. I should have been afraid of seeming to distribute false notes and to prevent poor people, by putting them off with dubious hopes, from claiming their portion in this world. These things are substantial enough for us to talk about them, to live by them, to think of them always; but they are not certain enough to enable us to be sure that in pretending to teach them we are not mistaken as to the quality of the goods delivered." Theophrastus, who discourses on "Probabilities," takes, on the whole, a cheerful view of the future —it must be confessed with considerable abatements. He agrees probably in a great measure with Theoctistes, who remarks, "I have never said that the future was cheerful. Who knows whether the truth is not sad?" Theophrastus thinks that the maturity of the world is to arrive by the expansion of science—on condition, indeed, that the mechanical theory of heat succeeds within five or six hundred years in inventing a substitute for coal. If it fails—and the failure is quite probable—"humanity will enter into a sort of mediocrity from which she will hardly have the means to emerge." It must be added that Theophrastus is prepared to see art and beauty (as we have hitherto understood them) disappear; "the day will perhaps come (we already see its dawn) when a great artist, a virtuous man, will be antiquated, almost useless things."

The speculations of Theoctistes, however, are much the most curious. He imagines a development of science so infinite and immeasurable that it will extend our relations beyond the limits of the planet on which we dwell, and he deems the function of this perfected machine to be above all the production of great men. The great men may be so selected and sifted and improved that human perfection may at last concentrate itself in one extremely superior being, who will hold all the universe in cheerful and grateful subordination. This is what Theoctistes calls "God being realized." With these sentiments it is not surprising that he should not expect that God will be realized by a democracy. He gets into deeper water than he can always buffet, but his style is the perfection of expression. I must quote a few lines more. "For myself, I relish the universe through that sort of general sentiment to which we owe it that we are sad in a sad city, gay in a gay city. I enjoy thus the pleasures of those given up to pleasure, the debauchery of the debauchee, the worldliness of the worldling, the holiness of the virtuous man, the meditations of the savant, the austerity of the ascetic. By a sort of sweet sympathy I imagine to myself that I am their consciousness. The discoveries of the savant are my property; the triumphs of the ambitious are my festival. I should be sorry that anything should be missing in this world, for I have the consciousness of all that it contains. My only displeasure is that the age has fallen so low that it no longer knows how to enjoy. Then I take refuge in the past—in the sixteenth century, in the seventeenth, in antiquity; everything that has been beautiful, amiable, noble, just, makes a sort of paradise for me. With this I defy misfortune to touch me; I carry with me the charming garden of the variety of my thoughts." This paragraph seems to me magnificent; one would like to have written it. The charm of M. Renan's style is hard to define; it is ethereal as a perfume. It is a style above all things urbane, and, with its exquisite form, is suggestive of moral graces, amenity, delicacy, generosity. Now that Sainte-Beuve is dead, it strikes me as the most perfect vehicle of expression actually in operation in France. The only style to be compared to it is that of Mme. Sand; but for pure quality even this must yield the palm. Mme. Sand's style is, after all (with all respect), a woman's style.

The much expected funeral of Michelet,[2] which took place ten days ago, may not, I suppose, be spoken of as an event of the hour; inasmuch as it conspicuously turned out not to be an event. To keep it from being an event was the earnest desire of Mme. Michelet and her friends, and it was feared that the large body of injudicious persons always on the lookout for chances to "manifest," radically, would take conflicting views, and that the highly unbecoming scenes which accompanied the recent interment of Mme. Louis Blanc—an Englishwoman and a Protestant—would be repeated. Mme. Michelet desired a secular, but not a political funeral. It may be remembered that she had just concluded, victoriously, a prolonged, painful and awkward contest with her husband's family touching the possession of his remains. They were finally adjudged to her, and she repaired to Cannes (where Michelet died, and where his relatives desired him to be buried) to bring them to Paris and consign them honorably to the soil in which there was an impressive fitness in their reposing. An immense concourse of people followed the body to the grave, but there was perfect order and no manifestation. Good taste, doubtless, for many excellent reasons, is not always a "radical" virtue; but on this occasion it was not wanting. It characterized especially the very eloquent address made at the grave by M. Challemel-Lacour,[3] who as speaker had long since won his spurs in the Assembly. His eulogy of Michelet was a very happy combination of passion and reason. Quietly as it was effected, however, the transfer to Paris of the great historian's remains has made Michelet again one of the subjects of the day, and the critics are revising and summing up their judgments of him. The *Revue des Deux Mondes* has just begun the publication of an extended essay on the subject by young M. d'Haussonville,[4] the author of the series of clever and somewhat perfidious papers upon Sainte-Beuve which appeared more than a year ago in the same pages. He will apparently treat Michelet more sympathetically—and it is rather odd he should, considering his highly conservative affiliations (M. d'Haussonville is nephew of the Duke de Broglie, and great-grandson of Mme. de Staël,[5] who certainly, if she were now living, would not be a Republican). In talking of Sainte-Beuve he made a very handsome show of generosity, but in turning the page one always found that he took back with one hand what he had given with the other. His account of Michelet's early life is extremely interesting; the great historian was a child of the people, in the narrowest sense of the term. His father was a small, struggling, unsuccessful printer, and Michelet's early years were spent in a damp cellar, setting up types with his little chapped hands. His whole youth was a time of poverty and hard obstruction, and on this point M. d'Haussonville quotes a few lines from a retrospect of Michelet which are well worth repeating: "I remember that this consummate misfortune, privations in the present, fears for the future, the enemy being but two steps off (1814), and my own personal enemies making daily sport of me, one day—one Thursday morning, I turned back upon myself without fire, with the snow covering everything, and my bread for the evening uncertain—I turned back upon myself, and without the least mixture of religious hope, had a pure feeling of stoicism; I struck with my hand, split open by the cold, upon my oaken table (which I have kept ever since), and felt a virile joy in my youth and my future."

In comparison with Michelet's early struggles to climb the ladder of knowledge, it may seem that such a career as that of Mme. Plessy, who has just bidden farewell to the stage at the Théâtre Français, offers but a trivial interest, but certainly nothing that is thoroughly well done has been easily done, and I am sure that the extraordinary perfection of Mme. Plessy's art was the fruit of a great deal of labor. Her last appearance the other night was a very brilliant solemnity. She acted portions of three or four of her most successful parts, and in conclusion, with the whole company of the Comédie Française gathered about her, she declaimed some very good verses by M. Sully-Pru-

dhomme.[6] She is a really irreparable loss to the stage,
which in spite of her advanced age she might for some
time have continued to adorn. Her age was not seriously perceptible; she is fifty-seven years old and had belonged to the Théâtre Français from her fifteenth year.
In 1845 she seceded, without ceremony, and repaired to
Russia, where she enjoyed fame and fortune for some
ten years. In 1855 she returned to the Comédie Française, quite *une princesse*, making her own terms and
paying none of the fines and penalties to which she had
been legally condemned. Since then, from year to year,
her talent has been growing richer and more perfect,
and it has now a blooming maturity which might long
bid defiance to time. The especially regrettable point
is that her place will probably never be filled, for she
was the last depositary of certain traditions which can
never, in the nature of things, be renewed. She was the
perfect great lady of high comedy, as high comedy
was possible before the invention of slang. She represented certain instincts and practices which have passed
out of manners. The other night, as she finished her
verses, she took Mlles. Sarah Bernhardt and Croizette
by the hands, and, with admirable grace, presented
them to the public as her substitutes. It is more than
likely that she had measured the irony of her gesture;
for from the moment it takes two actresses to make up
a Mme. Plessy, the cause is obviously lost. Clever as
those young ladies are, they will not fill the void. Their
art is small art; Mme. Plessy's was great art.

There are more exhibitions, but these also are small

art. The customary congregation of the "Refusés" [7] of
the Salon has gathered itself at Durand-Ruel's; but I
think it can have inflicted no twinges of conscience
upon the jury of admission. It is a melancholy collection of what are called in Parisian phrase *croûtes*—
crusts. It occasionally happens, among the "Refusés,"
that the verdict of the public helps a young painter to
his revenge upon the stony-hearted Cerberi of the
Salon; but this year the most sentimental admirer of
lost causes can find no pretext for enthusiasm. The
best things, by far, are a couple of native landscapes
by an American—Mr. J. Fairman. [8] (There is no harm
in printing his name, as it is in the catalogue and on
the frames of his pictures.) They are clever, but I understand very well why a French jury should have refused them. More interesting was the exhibition of
architectural projects for the Exhibition of 1878,
which was lately open for a few days at the École des
Beaux Arts. Architectural drawings, to the uninitiated,
are so much darkness visible; but the two or three main
conditions of the Exhibition are such as to help one to
infuse a certain picturesqueness into the diagrams. The
buildings are to stand on the Champ de Mars, as before, but there is now to be a great structure thrown
across the Seine, with the Pont d'Iéna for its founda-
tion, and the opposite hill of the Trocadéro is to be
covered with the dependencies of the show. It will be a
chance for the French genius for complex arrangement
to surpass itself. The architects and economists wish
greatly, I believe, that the Exhibition were to take

place three or four years later, and so, from the bottom of their hearts, do all quiet Parisians, native or adoptive. The only people who are in a hurry are the restaurateurs and the cab drivers.

HENRY JAMES, JR.

June 17, 1876

17

PARISIAN TOPICS

Letter from Henry James, Jr.

THE LATE M. DOUDAN'S CORRESPONDENCE—M. WADDING-
TON'S UNIVERSITY BILL—A BRILLIANT SEASON OF ITAL-
IAN OPERA—VERDI'S "AÏDA" AND "REQUIEM" PER-
FORMED—THE LATE GEORGE SAND

[FROM A REGULAR CORRESPONDENT OF THE "TRIBUNE"]

PARIS, June 9.—To people who are fond of good
letters I recommend those of the late M. Doudan,[1]
which have just been published by the Comte d'Haussonville, one of his principal correspondents. Good letters are the most entertaining reading (to my sense)
in the world, and in these two (it must be confessed
rather formidably massive) volumes this branch of literature, so exceptionally rich in France, has received
a delightful accession. M. Doudan was not known to
fame, and his letters will not make him famous, inasmuch as their interest is of a very tranquil order and
their charm of a sort to be appreciated only by people
of delicate taste, who are always in the minority. But
they are very exquisite and they testify eloquently to
the culture, the intelligence, and the intellectual good

manners of the circle of which their author was a member, and of which they form, as it were, simply the written conversations. M. Doudan was one of those men (everyone has known a specimen) whose friends speak of them and their powers in superlative terms, but whom, as there is little to show for these same powers, the outside world must take on trust—the men of whom, to the end of their days, it is said that they might do great things if they only would. They pass away without having done anything, and the brutal world shrugs its shoulders and observes that when people *can* do something, they manage sooner or later to do it, and that if a man stands all his life on the brink of the stream it is safe to conclude that he does not know how to swim. Sainte-Beuve somewhere speaks of M. Doudan as one of the *"suprêmes délicats"* whose ideal is placed so high that they give up ever trying to reach it. A great many clever men doubtless belong in this category, as well as a great many charlatans; but we must not forget the homely proverb which says that to make an omelet you must break your eggs. To write a good book one must hang one's ideal on a peg where one can reach it. M. Doudan passed the greater part of his life in the family of Broglie, to which he had been introduced through being engaged as preceptor to young M. de Rocca, the son of Mme. de Staël by her second marriage. He was an intimate friend of the Duchess de Broglie, the daughter of Mme. de Staël; I believe that this lady was a saint, and that the intimacy was observed to go as far as an intimacy between a saint and an agreeable man may go. His correspondents in these volumes are chiefly her children and her son-in-law, M. d'Haussonville. The letters range from the year 1827 to the year 1872, the period of the author's death; many of them, year after year, are dated from that charming château of Coppet, on the Lake of Geneva, in which Mme. de Staël spent her years of exile, and to which her descendants have continued to resort. M. Doudan was pre-eminently a literary man; literature was his passion, and two thirds of his allusions in these volumes are to books; but he wrote very little and published less—the editor informing us that even his *magnum opus*, a brief and extremely condensed treatise on the art of style and the principles of literary composition, which he had spent a great deal of time in polishing and perfecting, never left his portfolio. I believe, however, that it is now to be given to the world. I don't know what M. Doudan's theories were, but his practice is admirable. His own style is charming and the amount of excellent, of exquisite writing buried in these essentially familiar letters may excite the surprise of a generation whose epistolary manner threatens to savor more and more of the telegram and the postal card. There are letters and letters; those of M. Doudan are decidedly "old-fashioned," but they are not in the least ponderous. They are not formal dissertations on the one hand, nor on the other are they marked by the desperate vivacity of many of those social scribes who know that their letters are to be read aloud and handed about. They touch upon everything—events of the day,

people, books, abstract questions; some readers will
perhaps complain that they contain too little gossip,
and absolutely no scandal. They have a great deal of
humor, pitched in the minor key; it is never quite absent, but it never rises to the height (or sinks to the
depth) of the comic. I had marked a great many passages for quotation, but I must use the privilege scant-
ily. Every now and then there is something excellently
said—as when, speaking of foreign literatures, and de-
claring that one never really enters into them, or cares
to enter into them, as the natives do, that they have
always a strangeness for us, M. Doudan affirms that
"at bottom there are only two things that really please
us, the ideal or our own likeness." Excellent, too, is this
about Rousseau: "I am not surprised that he has dis-
pleased you. There is nothing sadder to see than this
lively imagination, with its strength and severity, gov-
erned by vulgar inclinations. He wished sincerely to live
according to the ideal which he saw floating before him,
but his nature rebelling too strongly, he squeezed into
his ideal all the pitiable qualities of his personal nature, by conscience, by insanity, and also by a certain
perversity." And St. Augustine, he adds (whom his
correspondent appears also to have been reading), "his
confessions make one think of everything. They are
like a fine night of Africa. Great shadows, vast spaces,
and the eternal stars." M. Doudan had, as a young
man, paid a short visit to Italy, and his Italian memories kept him company for life. His allusions to Italian things are constant, and they have an almost pas-

sionate tenderness. "A young Roman girl of the bourgeoisie has her confessor lodging behind St. Peter's, and in passing she thinks neither of the dome of St. Peter's, nor of the Egyptian obelisk, nor of the statues of Bernini, nor of the lions of Canova; but all these things are mingled confusedly with her real life. She is a bright little flower on the walls of a great monument. The sun of Rome has given her her brightness, but she doesn't know it. An old English lady declaims as she gazes on the Roman horizon, the catacombs, and the pines of the Villa Pamfili; and while the old English lady remains ugly and pale and declamatory, the little Roman bourgeoise, who has never been so wise, grows up and becomes beautiful without thinking of the Tarquins or the Gracchi. M. de Langsdorf," he adds, "means soon to sail; but for my part, fond as I am of nature, I shouldn't care to go into those unsettled parts of America. I would rather see Königsberg or Nuremberg, under their grey sky, than all those virgin forests which have never been looked at but by lumber dealers. I am like my old English lady of just now: I like to declaim over old times, but if today I could be eighteen years old and have been born in Rome, even in the Via Babuino, I would give up forever all present and future declamations. But you can't be eighteen for wishing it, and if ever I am eighteen again I shall stay so." A short time before the Roman revolution of 1848 he writes: "I lay my curse in advance upon all Italians who are not of an extreme moderation in these hard days. But patience and modera-

tion are rare virtues. I don't know why they give the
name of hero to those who mount a ladder under fire
and plant a flag on a wall in the midst of balls. It's a
matter of half an hour, after which you may go and lie
down on a bed of laurels freshly cut. It is only those
who have real patience and moderation who should be
called heroes. Those are the great battles—battles that
last long. You have to lie for years on peach kernels,
with doubt on your right hand and on your left the
crowd, who informs you that you have no blood in your
veins, and to ascertain it, wants every now and then to
cut your throat." Lastly—apropos of M. Renan's brilliant first literary performances: "The truth is he is
like a young colt; he is fond of kicking up his heels.
. . . A man must certainly have some vague ideas; a
clever man who has none but clear ones is a fool, who
will never come to anything; but nevertheless there
must be some solid bones to hold a living being together
when he is not of the race of the snakes. I don't see M.
Renan's bones." M. Doudan's letters, in short, present
an interesting image of a quiet, sensitive, fastidious
man, living by preference on the shady side of life, possessing the most delicate perceptions and tastes, as well
as the most agreeable culture, but haunted by a melancholy sense of his ineffectiveness. His gaiety is subdued; there is a cast of autumnal haze in his sunshine.
I may add that he appears to have been a voracious
reader of English books, and to have had, in particular, an insatiable appetite for British fiction. On this
last point he was a flattering exception to his country-

men; most French people to whom I have spoken of English novels have made up a very wry face.

Of what is going on in the lighter realms of Parisian activity there is no very brilliant account to give. People are, of course, thinking and talking much of the dark clouds in the East,[2] but this cannot at the best be classed among "light" subjects. M. Waddington has just succeeded in putting through his bill restricting to the state the power of conferring university degrees —a sensible defeat to the Catholic party. But neither is this a light theme. The *fauteuil* of M. Guizot at the Academy has just been taken possession of by his successor, M. Dumas, the distinguished chemist and physicist.[3] I am at a loss to perceive on what grounds M. Dumas has sought a place in a purely literary body; but in his *discours de réception* he paid a great many compliments to literature as well as to M. Guizot—so many that stern science, I should think, would feel a trifle jilted. I sometimes feel inclined to exclaim, in emulation of Mme. Roland, "Oh, Académie Française, what crimes are committed in thy name!" There is nothing new of consequence at the theaters, and some of them are about to close. I should like, however, in so far as a strictly nonmusical auditor has a right to speak of such a matter, to say a good word for the brilliant short season of Italian opera which is just coming to an end at the Salle Ventadour. Verdi's *Aïda* and the same master's lately composed *Requiem*[4] have been the only works performed, but they have been given with great perfection and proportionate success. The sing-

ers have been the great composer's own and peculiar
quartet—Mmes. Stoltz and Waldmann, and, as tenor
and baritone, MM. Masini and Medini. I don't know
when I have partaken of such a feast of vocalism. The
voice of Mme. Stoltz is phenomenal; it seems to belong
to two persons. If you shut your eyes when she passes
from one end of her register to the other you are ready
to swear that a second singer has intervened. The liquid
contralto of Mlle. Waldmann is most enchanting, but
the prize, to my sense, belongs to the admirable tenor
of M. Masini, which seems to contain the very soul of
youth and tenderness. It is deemed to be, I believe, a
very vivid echo of Mario. It is the ideal voice of one's
twentieth year; if that time of life could always sing, it
would sing just so. I will not profess to have enjoyed
very profusely the somewhat obstreperous (from the
Italian point of view exotic) music of *Aïda*, but I found
the *Requiem* in places irresistibly moving—the more so
that Signor Verdi himself stood there, conducting the
orchestra with a certain passionate manner. In the way
of further gossip of this class, there has been the dis-
tribution of the prizes at the Salon, and the bestowal
of the medal of honor upon the two figures in sculpture of M. Paul Dubois, of which I lately made appreciative mention. Never was an honor better earned,
and never can it have been adjudged with more un-
grudging unanimity. I have it at heart to add that the
two fantastic pictures of M. Gustave Moreau, to which
I made but a cursory allusion, the "Hercules and the
Hydra of Ternos" and the "Salomé," have proved the

lions of the Salon. I confess that, with myself, they have greatly improved on acquaintance. They are very remarkable, full of imagination, and if not of first-class power at least of first-class subtlety.

Since I began my letter the news has come of a great loss to literature—the death of George Sand.[5] She died in that rustic château of Nohant, in the old province of Berry, which she had so often and so picturesquely described. She had been painfully and alarmingly ill for a number of days, and the public was prepared for the event. It is the close of a very illustrious and very interesting career, of which I must defer speaking at length to my next writing. Mme. Sand is not, as was at first affirmed, to be buried at Paris, but at Nohant, to which (as I believe) somewhat inaccessible spot a numerous deputation from the literary world has piously repaired. It has been proposed, says the *Figaro*, to Alexandre Dumas to pronounce her funeral oration. I hope he will decline. Mme. Sand, admire her with what modification we will, deserves a better fate than to serve as a pretext for this gentleman's self-complacent epigrams. Mme. Sand was seventy-two years of age. She had of late lived almost exclusively in the country, and at the time of her death had not been to Paris for two winters. I have heard her this winter much spoken of by persons who knew her well, and always with great esteem. Her life had had many phases, but the longest was that of her old age, which was very tranquil and reasonable; so much so as to efface the memory of certain others which had preceded it, and which had been of a more questionable cast. She had always been a singular mixture of quietude and turbulence. I am told that she was fearfully shy; her books are certainly of all books the least shy. She had little conversation, and yet her books are singularly loquacious and confidential. Her fertility was most extraordinary, and her admirers will be anxious to learn whether it has not bequeathed some documents—memoirs, reminiscences, or narratives more explicitly fictitious—which are yet to see the light.

HENRY JAMES, JR.

July 1, 1876

18

GEORGE SAND

Letter from Henry James, Jr.

INCIDENTS OF HER CAREER——HER TIRELESS INDUSTRY——
M. RENAN'S TRIBUTE TO HER GENIUS——CHARACTERISTICS
OF HER EARLIER AND LATER WORKS

[FROM A REGULAR CORRESPONDENT OF THE "TRIBUNE"]

PARIS, June 28.——The newspapers, for the last fortnight, have contained a certain number of anecdotes
about Mme. Sand; [1] but they have been generally of a
rather trivial sort, and I have not gathered any that
are worth repeating. Private life in France——more for-
tunate than among ourselves——is still acknowledged to
have some rights which the reporter and the interviewer
are bound to respect. A Frenchman often makes surprising confidences to the public about himself, but as
a rule he is not addicted to telling tales about his
neighbor. Mme. Sand, in the memoirs which she published twenty years ago, lifted the veil from her personality with a tolerably unshrinking hand (though to
the admirers of what is called scandal she gave very
little satisfaction) ; and yet for the last thirty years of
her life, she was one of the most shade-loving and re-

tiring of celebrities. Her life, indeed, was almost entirely in her books, and it is there that one must look for it. She was essentially a scribbler; she wrote unceasingly from the publication of her first novel to the day of her death, and she had always been fond above all things of a quiet life, even during that portion of her career in which our Anglo-Saxon notions of "quietness" are supposed to have been most effectively violated. She was very intimate at one time with Alfred de Musset, and I have heard that this charming poet, by right of his membership in the *genus irritabile,* sometimes found it more than his nerves could endure to see the author of *Consuelo* sit down to her perpetual manuscript at the most critical hours of their somewhat troubled friendship. But Mme. Sand wrote for her bread, and her remarkable power of imaginative abstraction must help to explain the very large amount of work that she achieved. She was also very intimate with Prosper Mérimée, and I have been told that very early one cold winter morning he perceived her, with a handkerchief on her head, lighting the fire to resume her literary tasks. He also, it appears, had nerves; the spectacle disturbed them—he himself was not thinking of getting about his labors yet awhile—and from that moment the intimacy ceased. Mme. Sand had spent a large portion of her life at Nohant, in the Berry, in the plain old country house which she described so charmingly in *L'Histoire de Ma Vie,* and for which and for its (I believe) rather meager setting of natural beauty she appears to have had a singularly intense affection. As she advanced in life, Nohant became more and more her home, and her visits to Paris were brief. Her house was very hospitable, and under her own roof she was never without society. She had worked very hard, and she had made no fortune; she still earned her income—an income which at the bottom, as they say, of an old French province is still considered easy, but which in America, as in England, would not be thought in fair proportion to the writer's industry and eminence. Mme. Sand made, I believe, between six and seven thousand dollars a year. She was very silent, and had little assurance of manner. People who knew her well have told me that she looked a great deal on the ground, and seemed preoccupied; that one felt shut off from her by a sort of veil or film. Occasionally this veil was lifted, she found her voice, and talked to very good purpose. This characterization corresponds with a phrase which one of her heroes, in I forget what novel, applies to one of her heroines—the heroine being an idealized portrait of Mme. Sand herself. He calls her a *sphinx bon enfant*—"a good-natured sphinx." In spite of her advanced age—she was seventy-two—Mme. Sand's vigor had not failed at the time of the sudden illness which ended in her death. Her activity was great, and her faculties unimpaired. I saw a letter, the other day, written a few weeks before she died, in which she declared that her eyesight was better than when she was fifty, and that she went upstairs as fast as her dog. She was carried off by an acute attack of a malady which she had at first neglected. Her last audible words on her deathbed were characteristic of one who had loved nature passionately, and described it almost incomparably—"Laissez verdure." The allusion was apparently to some wild herbage in the corner of the village churchyard in which she expressed a wish to rest. In spite of her complete rupture, early in life, with Catholicism—in spite of *Spiridion, Mademoiselle La Quintinie,* and numberless other expressions of religious independence—Mme. Sand was buried from the little church of Nohant, and the curé performed the service. Her family had the good taste to ask permission of the Bishop of Bourges, and the Bishop had the good taste to answer that if she had not positively refused the sacraments he saw no objection. What made it good taste in Mme. Sand's family (it was poor logic) was the fact that she was greatly beloved by the country people, that she had been held in great esteem by the prior generation, that these people were numerically her chief mourners, and that it would have perplexed and grieved them not to see her buried in the only fashion of which they recognized the impressiveness. Alexandre Dumas did not pronounce a funeral oration, though he was, with Prince Napoleon, one of the pallbearers. A short address by Victor Hugo was read—he not being personally present. It had all of his latter-day magniloquence, but it contained no phrase so happy in its eloquence as one that I find in a letter from Ernest Renan, published in the *Temps* a few days after Mme. Sand's death. The last lines she had written were a short notice of M. Renan's new book, the

Dialogues Philosophiques. "I am touched to the bottom of my heart," he says, "to have been the last to produce a vibration of that sonorous soul which was, as it were, the Aeolian harp of our time." Persons who have read Mme. Sand with a certain amount of sympathy will find it just, as well as fanciful, to call her soul "sonorous." It is an excellent description of her intellectual temperament. A few other fine lines in M. Renan's letter are worth quoting: "Mme. Sand went through all visions, smiled at them all, believed in them all; her practical judgment may occasionally have gone astray, but as an artist she never deceived herself. Her works are truly the echo of our age. When this poor nineteenth century which we abuse so much is gone, it will be heard and eagerly looked into, and much one day will be forgiven it. George Sand then will rise up as our interpreter. The age has not had a wound with which her heart has not bled, not an ailment of which she has not harmoniously complained." I suspect that M. Renan has not perused any very great number of Mme. Sand's fictions, but this is none the less very finely said.

I have been refreshing my memory of some of George Sand's earlier novels, which I confess I do not find as easy reading as I once did. But—taking the later ones as well—they are a very extraordinary and splendid series, and certainly one of the great literary achievements of our time. Some people, I know, cannot read Mme. Sand; she has no illusion for them and but a moderate amount of charms; but I think such people

are to be pitied—they lose a great pleasure. She was
an *improvisatrice,* raised to a very high power; she
told stories as a nightingale sings. No novelist answers
so well to the childish formula of "making up as you
go along." Other novels seem meditated, pondered,
calculated, thought out, and elaborated with a certain
amount of trouble; but the narrative with Mme. Sand
always appears to be an invention of the moment, flow-
ing from a mind which a constant process of quiet contemplation, absorption, and revery keeps abundantly
supplied with material. It is a sort of general emana-
tion, an intellectual evaporation. There had been plenty
of improvisation before the author of *Consuelo,* but
it had never been—and it has never been in other hands
—of so fine a quality. She had a natural gift of style
which is certainly one of the most remarkable of our
day; her diction from the first was ripe and flexible,
and seemed to have nothing to learn from practice. The
literary form of her writing has always been exquisite;
and this alone would have sufficed to distinguish it
from the work of the great body of clever scribblers
who spin their two or three plots a year. Some of her
novels are very inferior to others; some of them show
traces of weariness, of wandering attention, of a care-
less choice of subject; but the manner, at the worst,
never sinks below a certain high level—the tradition
of good writing is never lost. In this bright, voluminous
envelope, it must be confessed that Mme. Sand has
sometimes wrapped up a rather flimsy kernel; some of
her stories will not bear much thinking over. But her

great quality from the first was the multiplicity of her interests and the activity of her sympathies. She passed through a succession of phases, faiths, and doctrines—political, religious, moral, social, personal—and to each she gave a voice which the conviction of the moment made eloquent. She gave herself up to each as if it were to be final, and in every case she turned her steps behind her. Sainte-Beuve, who as an artist relished her but slenderly, says somewhere, in allusion to her, that "no one had ever played more fairly and openly at the great game of life." It has been said wittily, in reference to Buffon's well-known axiom, that "the style is the man" (which by the way is a misquotation), that of no one was this dictum ever so true as of Mme. Sand; but I incline to believe, with the critic in whose pages I find this *mot*, that at bottom the man was always Mme. Sand herself. She accepted as much of every influence as suited her, and when she had written a novel or two about it she ceased to care about it. This proves her, doubtless, to have been a decidedly superficial moralist; but it proves her to have been a born romancer. It is by the purely romantic side of her productions that she will live. It is a misfortune that she pretended to moralize to the extent that she did, for about moral matters her head was not at all clear. It had now and then capital glimpses and inspirations, but her didacticism has always seemed to me what an architectural drawing would be, executed by a person who should turn up his nose at geometry. Mme. Sand's straight lines are straight by a happy chance—and for people of genius there are so many happy chances. She was without a sense of certain differences—the difference between the pure and the impure—the things that are possible for people of a certain delicacy, and the things that are not. When she struck the right notes, and so long as she continued to strike them, the result was charming, but a sudden discord was always possible. Sometimes the right note was admirably prolonged—as for instance in her masterpiece, *Consuelo,* in which during three long volumes, if I remember rightly, the charming heroine adheres strictly to the straight line. After all, Mme. Sand's "tendency" novels, as the Germans call such works, constitute but the minor part of her literary bequest; as she advanced in life she wrote her stories more and more for the story's sake, and attempted to prove nothing more alarming than that human nature is on the whole tolerably noble and generous. After this pattern she produced a long list of masterpieces. Her imagination seemed gifted with perpetual youth; the freshness of her invention was marvelous. Her novels have a great many faults; they lack three or four qualities which the realistic novel of the last thirty or forty years, with its great successes, has taught us to consider indispensable. They are not exact nor probable; they contain few living figures; they produce a limited amount of illusion. Mme. Sand created no figures that have passed into common life and speech; her people are usually only very picturesque, very voluble, and very "high-toned" shadows. But the shadows move to such a persuasive music that we watch them with interest. The art of narration is extraordinary. This was Mme. Sand's great art. The recital moves along with an evenness, a lucidity, a tone of seeing, feeling, knowing everything, a reference to universal things, a sentimental authority, which makes the reader care for the characters in spite of his incredulity and feel anxious about the story in spite of his impatience. He feels that the author holds in her hands a stringed instrument composed of the chords of the human soul.

Paris is settling herself for her summer siesta, and all disturbing sounds are daily growing fainter. There is indeed a vague booming of cannon, actual and prospective, beyond the eastern horizon, and her sleep may have troubled dreams. The race for the Grand Prix came off some three weeks ago, and the Grand Prix, I believe, is the high-water mark of Parisian animation. Since then the tide has rapidly ebbed. I have left myself no space to speak—how profanely soever—of this equine contest, and I have the opportunity to devote but a few lines to the Review of the 15th of June. I witnessed the latter ceremony from a rickety straw-bottomed chair, upon which I stood for three or four hours in a very hot sun; but in spite of my discomfort I thought the Review entertaining—which is speaking handsomely. It was held on the immense race grounds at Longchamp, and consisted of a simple march past of 40,000 troops or so stationed in Paris or immediately near it. The day was charming, and the crowd enormous, and Marshal MacMahon and his staff and escort formed a very glittering array. The little red legs seemed to me to march very neatly, and the artillery to thunder by with a proper amount of method in its madness; the dragoons and cuirassiers, on the other hand, did not strike me as sitting their horses like the young Greeks on the friezes of the Parthenon. But the whole show, I believe, was pronounced creditable, and, asking no oversearching questions of it, I was quite willing to exclaim, with the Grand Duchess of Gérolstein—*"Ah, que j'aime les militaires!"*

HENRY JAMES, JR.
July 22, 1876

19

SUMMER IN FRANCE [1]

Letter from Henry James, Jr.

PARIS IN SUMMERTIME—FESTIVE ASPECT OF THE BOULE-
VARDS—DINING AT AUTEUIL AND AT THE BOIS—THE
ATLANTIC AT HAVRE—THE CATHEDRAL IN ROUEN—THE
CHURCH OF ST. OUEN

[FROM A REGULAR CORRESPONDENT OF THE "TRIBUNE"]

————————— ◆ —————————

HAVRE, July 22.—It is quite in the nature of things
that a Parisian correspondence should have flagged
during the last few weeks; for even the most brilliant
of capitals, when the summer has fairly marked her
for its own, affords few topics to the chronicler. To
a chronicle of small beer such a correspondence almost
literally finds itself reduced. The correspondent con-
sumes a goodly number of these narrow mugfuls of
this fluid, known in Paris as "bocks," and from the
shadiest corner of the coolest café he can discover
watches the glaring asphalt grow more largely inter-
spaced. There is little to do or to see, and therefore
little to write about. There is in fact only one thing
to do, namely, to get out of Paris. The lively imagination of the correspondent anticipates his departure and

takes its flight to one of the innumerable watering
places whose charms at this season are set forth in
large yellow and pink placards affixed to all the empty
walls. They order this matter, like so many others,
much better in France. Here you have not, as with us,
to hunt up the "summer retreat" about which you desire information in a dense alphabetical list in the columns of a newspaper; you are familiar with its merits
for three weeks before you start—you have seen them
half a dozen times a day emblazoned along the line of
your customary walk, as vivid and substantial as the
hand and seal of the corporation of the Casino can
make them. If you are detained in Paris, however, after
luckier mortals have departed—your reflections upon
the fate of the luckless mortals who do not depart at
all are quite another question, demanding another
chapter—I don't know that it makes you much happier
to peruse these high-toned posters, which seem to flut-
ter with the breezes of Houlgate and Étretat. You must
take your consolation where you can find it, and it
must be added that of all great cities Paris is the most
tolerable in hot weather. It is true that the asphalt
has a way of liquefying to about the consistency and
the temperature of molten lava, and it is true that the
brilliant limestone of which the city is built reflects the
sun with uncomfortable fierceness. It is also true that
of a summer evening you pay a penalty for living in
the best lighted capital in the world. The inordinate
amount of gas in all the thoroughfares heats and thick-
ens the atmosphere, and makes you feel of a July night

as if you were in a vast concert hall. If you look down at such a time upon the central portions of Paris from a high window in a remoter quarter, you see them wrapped in a sort of lurid haze of the devil's own brewing. But, on the other hand, there are a hundred persuasions to keeping out of doors. You are not obliged to sit on a "stoop" or on a curbstone, as in New York. The boulevards are a long chain of cafés, each one with its little promontory of chairs and tables projecting into the sea of asphalt. These promontories are doubtless not exactly islands of the blessed, peopled though some of them may be with sirens addicted to beer, but they may help you to pass a hot evening. Then you may dine in the Champs Élysées at a table spread under the trees, beside an ivied wall, and almost believe you are in the country. This illusion, imperfect as it is, is a luxury and must be paid for accordingly; the dinner is not so good as at a restaurant on the boulevard, and is considerably dearer, and there is after all not much difference in sitting with one's feet in dusty gravel or on a sanded floor. But the whole situation is more idyllic. I indulged in a cheap idyl the other day by taking the penny steamer down the Seine to Auteuil (a very short sail), and dining at what is called in Parisian parlance a *guinguette* on the bank of the stream. It was a very humble style of entertainment, but the most frantic pursuit of pleasure can do no more than succeed, and this was a success. The Seine at Auteuil is wide and is spanned by a stately viaduct of two tiers of arches, which stands up against the sky

in a picturesque and monumental manner. Your table
is spread under a trellis which scratches your head—
spread chiefly with fried fish—and an old man who
looks like a very high-toned political exile comes and
stands before it and sings a doleful ditty on the respect
due to white hairs. You testify by the bestowal of a
couple of coppers to the esteem with which his own
inspire you, and he is speedily replaced by a lad with
one arm, who treats you to something livelier: "*À la
bonne heure; parlez-moi de ça!*"

You eventually return to Paris on the top of a
horsecar. It is a very different affair to go out and
dine at the Bois de Boulogne, at the charming restaurant which is near the cascade and the Longchamp race
course. Here are no ballad singers, but stately trees
picturesquely grouped, and making long evening shadows on a lawn, and irreproachable tables, and carriages
rolling up behind high-stepping horses, and depositing
all sorts of ladies. The drive back through the wood at
night is most charming, and the coolness of the air extreme, however hot you may be still certain to find the
city.

The best thing, therefore, is not to go back. I write
these lines at an inn at Havre, before a window which
frames the picture of the seaward path of the transatlantic steamers. One of the great black ships is at this
moment painted on the canvas, very near, and beginning
its outward journey. I watch it to the right-hand ledge
of the window, which is as far as a poor sailor need
be expected to follow it. The hotel at Havre is called,

for mysterious reasons, Frascati—reasons which I give up the attempt to fathom, so undiscoverable are its points of analogy with the lovely village of the same name which nestles among the olives of the Roman hills. The locality has its charms, however. It is very agreeable, for instance, at the end of a hot journey, to sit down to dinner in a great open cage, hung over the Atlantic, and, while the sea breeze cools your wine, watch the swiftly moving ships pass before you like the figures on the field of a magic lantern. It is pleasant also to open your eyes in the early dawn, before the light is intense, and without moving your head on the pillow, enjoy the same clear outlook on the ocean highway. In the vague dusk, with their rapid gliding, the sailing vessels look like the ghosts of wrecked ships. Most seaports are picturesque, and Havre is not the least so; but my enjoyment has been not of my goal, but of my journey. My head is full of the twenty-four hours I have just passed at Rouen, and of the charming sail down the Seine to Honfleur. Rouen is a city of very ancient renown, and yet I confess I was not prepared to find so magnificent a little town.[2] The traveler who treads the Rouen streets at the present day sees but the shadow of their former picturesqueness; for the broom of M. Haussmann has swept through the city, and a train of "embellishments" has followed in its track. The streets have been widened and straightened, and the old houses—gems of medieval domestic architecture—which formed the peculiar treasure of the city, have been more than decimated.

A great deal remains, however—to American eyes a very great deal. The cathedral, the churches, and the Palais de Justice are alone a splendid group of monuments, and a stroll through the streets reveals a collection of brown and sculptured façades, of quaintly timbered gables, of curious turrets and casements and doorways, which still may be called rich. Every now and then a good long stretch of duskiness and crookedness delights the sentimental traveler, who is to pass but a couple of nights at Rouen, and who does not care if his favorite adjective is balanced with another epithet also beginning with a *p*. It is nothing to him that the picturesque is pestiferous. It is everything to him that the great front of the cathedral is magnificently battered, and heavy, and impressive. It has been defaced on a vast scale, and is now hardly more than a collection of empty niches. I do not mean, of course, that the wanton tourist rejoices in the absence of the statues which once filled them, but up to the present moment, at least, he is not sorry that the façade has not been restored. It consists of a sort of screen, pierced in the center with a huge wheel window, crowned with a pyramid of chiseled needles and spires, flanked with two turrets capped with tall empty canopies, and covered, generally, with sculptures—bas-relief, statues, and ornaments. On each side of it rise two great towers, one a rugged mass of early Norman work, with little ornament save its hatcheted closed arches, and its great naked base as huge and white as the bottom of a chalk cliff; the other a specimen of sixteenth-century gothic, extremely flamboyant and elegant and confounding to the eye. The sides of the cathedral are as yet more or less imbedded in certain black and dwarfish old houses, but if you pass around them by a long detour, you arrive at two superb lateral porches. The so-called Portail des Libraires, in especial, on the northern side, is a magnificent affair, sculptured from summit to base (it is now restored), and preceded by a long forecourt, in which the guild of booksellers used to hold its musty traffic. From here you can see the immense central tower, perched above the junction of the transepts and the nave, and crowned with a gigantic iron spire lately erected to replace one which was destroyed by lightning in the early part of the century. This gaunt pyramid has the drawback, to American eyes, of resembling too much the tall fire towers which are seen in transatlantic cities, and its dimensions are such that, viewed from a distance, it fairly makes little Rouen look top-heavy. Behind the choir within is a beautiful lady-chapel, and in this chapel are two enchanting works of art. The larger and more striking of these is the tomb of the two Cardinals d'Amboise,[3] uncle and nephew, the elder, if I mistake not, Minister of Francis I. It consists of a shallow, oblong recess in the wall, lined with gilded and fretted marble, and corniced with delicate little statues. Within the recess the figures of the two cardinals are kneeling with folded hands and ruggedly earnest faces, their long robes spread out behind them with magnificent amplitude. They are full of life, dignity, and piety; they look like

portraits of Holbein transmuted into marble. The base
of the monument is composed of a series of admirable
little images representing the cardinal and other virtues, and the effect of the whole work is admirably
grave and rich. The discreet traveler will never miss
an opportunity to come into a great church at eventide—the hour when his fellow travelers, less discreet,
are lingering over the table d'hôte, when the painted
windows glow with a deeper splendor, when the long
wand of the beadle, slowly tapping the pavement, or
the shuffle of the old sacristan, has a ghostly resonance
along the empty nave, and three or four work-weary
women, before a dusky chapel, are mumbling for the
remission of unimaginable sins. At this hour, at Rouen,
the tomb of the Duke de Brézé, husband of Diana of
Poitiers, placed opposite to the monument I have just
described, seemed to me the most beautiful thing in the
world. It is presumably the work of the charming sixteenth-century sculptor, Jean Ponjon, and it bears the
stamp of his graceful and inventive talent. The de-
ceased is lying on his back almost naked, with a part
of his shroud bound in a knot about his head—a realistic but not a repulsive image of death. At his head
kneels the amiable Diana, in sober garments, all decency and devotion; at his feet stands the Virgin, a
charming young woman with a charming child. Above,
on another tier, the subject of the monument is represented in the fullness of life, dressed as for a tournament, bestriding a high-stepping war horse, riding
forth like a Roland or a Galahad. The architecture of

the tomb is most graceful and the subordinate figures admirable, but the image of the dead Duke is altogether a masterpiece. The other evening, in the solemn stillness and the fading light of the great cathedral, it seemed irresistibly human and touching. The spectator felt a sort of impulse to smooth out the shroud and straighten the helpless hands.

The second church of Rouen, St. Ouen, the beautiful and harmonious, has no monuments of this value, but it offers within a higher interest than the cathedral. Without, it looks like an English abbey, scraped and restored, disencumbered of huddling neighbors and surrounded on three sides by a beautiful garden. Seen to this excellent advantage it is one of the noblest of churches; but within, it is one of the most fascinating. I am always, in architectural matters, very much of the opinion of the last speaker; the last fine building I have seen seems to me for the time the finest possible. This is deplorable levity; yet I risk the affirmation apropos of St. Ouen. I can imagine no more consummate combination of lightness and majesty. Its proportions bring tears to the eyes. I have left myself space only to recommend the sail down the Seine from Rouen to the mouth of the stream; but I recommend it in the highest terms. The heat was extreme and the little steamer most primitive, but the river is as picturesque as one could wish. It makes an infinite number of bends, and corners, and angles, rounded by a charming vegetation. Abrupt and rocky hills go with it all the way—hills with cornfields lying in their hollows, and forests crowning their tops. Out of the forests peep old manors, and beneath, between the hills and the stream, are high-thatched farmsteads, lying deep in their meadows and orchards, cottages palisaded with hollyhocks, gray old Norman churches, and villas shaded with enormous trees. It is a land of peace and plenty, and remarkable to Anglo-Saxon eyes for the English-looking details of its scenery. I noticed a hundred places where one might have been in Kent as well as in Normandy. In fact it is almost better than Kent, for Kent has no Seine. At the last the river becomes unmistakably an arm of the sea, and as a river, therefore, less interesting. But crooked little Honfleur, with its miniature port, clinging to the side of a cliff as luxuriant as one of the headlands of the Mediterranean, is a picturesque last incident.

HENRY JAMES, JR.
August 12, 1876

20

A FRENCH WATERING PLACE [1]

Letter from Henry James, Jr.

ÉTRETAT ON THE COAST OF NORMANDY—ITS SIMPLICITY
AND ATTRACTIONS—SCENERY—THE BLUFFS—CUSTOMS
OF VISITORS—JACQUES OFFENBACH

[FROM A REGULAR CORRESPONDENT OF THE "TRIBUNE"]

ÉTRETAT, Aug. 4.—The coast of Normandy and
Picardy, from Trouville to Boulogne, is a chain of
what the French call bathing stations, each with its
particular claim to patronage. The grounds of the
claim are in some cases not particularly obvious; but
they are generally found to reside in the fact that if
the locality is nasty, it is also cheap. There are the
places that are dear and brilliant, like Trouville and
Dieppe, and places that are cheap and dreary, like
Fécamp and Cabourg. Then there are the places that
are both cheap and pleasant. This delightful combination of qualities may be found in the modest *station
de bains* from which I write these lines. At Étretat you
may enjoy some of the finest cliff scenery it has been
my fortune to behold, and you may breakfast and dine
at the principal hotel for the sum of five and a half

francs a day. You may engage a room in the town over a butcher's shop, a tailor's or a laundress's at a rate that will depend upon your talent for driving a bargain, but that in no case will be exorbitant. Add to this your subscription to the Casino, which, for the season, will amount to some $8.00 or $9.00, your few coppers daily for the hire of your bathing toggery, and your matutinal subsidy to the lame beggar at the beginning of the beach, and you have a list of all your possible expenses at Étretat. You wear old clothes, you walk in canvas shoes, you deck your head with a fisherman's cap (when made of white flannel these articles may be extolled for their coolness, convenience, and picturesqueness), you lie on the pebbly strand most of the day, watching the cliffs, the waves, and the bathers; in the evening you loaf about the Casino, and you keep monkish hours. Though Étretat enjoys great and deserved popularity, I see no symptoms of the decline of these simple fashions—no menace of the invasion of luxury. A little more luxury, indeed, might be imported without doing any harm; though after all we soon learn that it is an idle enough prejudice that has hitherto prevented us from keeping our soap in a sugar dish and closing our clothes press with a stone. From a Parisian point of view, Étretat is certainly primitive, but it would be affectation on the part of an American to pretend that he was not agreeably surprised to find a "summer resort," in which he had been warned that he would have to rough it, so completely appointed and so intelligently organized.

Étretat may be primitive, but Étretat is French, and therefore Étretat is "administered." The place strikes me as a rather happy combination of smoothness and roughness. It weans you from the corruptions of civilization, but it lets you down gently upon the bosom of nature; it doesn't dump you there with the brutality observable upon the coast of Maine and of Massachusetts.

Étretat, like most of the French watering places, has a brief history. Twenty years ago it was but a cluster of fishing huts. A group of artists and literary people were its first colonists, and Alphonse Karr [2] became the mouthpiece of their enthusiasm. In vulgar phrase, he wrote up the place, and he lives in legend, at the present hour, as the *genius loci*. The main street is named after him; the gable of the chief inn—the classic Hôtel Blanquet—is adorned with a colored medallion representing his cropped head and long beard; the shops are stocked with his photographs and with pictures of his villa. I don't know whether, like the hero of Mrs. Shelley's *Frankenstein*, he became appalled at the monster he had created, and felt that he had succeeded too well; but of late years he has withdrawn from Étretat. The artistic fraternity, however, still haunt the place, and it enjoys also the favor of theatrical people, three or four of whom, having retired upon their laurels, possess villas here. The largest luminary in this line is M. Jacques Offenbach,[3] who, I believe, has for some time lived here, and who may be seen in the evenings in the Casino, sitting in quiet attitudes, and, to one's extreme surprise, not shaking his legs, making play with his eyes, or indulging in any degree in that familiar quality of gesticulation with which his name is so invariably associated. From my open window, as I write these lines, I look out and over a little cluster of clean housetops at the long green flank of the downs, as it slopes down to the town from the summit of the cliffs. To the right is the top of an old storm-twisted grove of oaks in the heart of which stands a picturesque farmhouse; then comes the sharp, even outline of the down, with its side spotted with little flat bushes and wrinkled with winding paths, along which, here and there, I see a bright figure moving; on the left, above the edge of the cliff, stands a bleak little chapel to our Lady of the fishing folk. Just here a most provoking chimney starts up and cuts off my view of the downward plunge of the cliff, showing me but a gleam of its white, fantastic profile, and a bar of blue ocean beside it. But there is not far to go to see without impediments. Three minutes' walk along the Rue Alphonse Karr, where every house is a shop, and every house has lodgers above it, who scramble bedward by a ladder and trapdoor, brings you to the little pebbly bay where the cliffs fall and the foreign life of Étretat goes forward. At one end are the small fishing smacks, with their green sides and their black sails, resting crookedly upon the stones; at the other is the Casino, and the two or three tiers of bathing houses on the slope of the beach in front of it. This beach may be said to be Étretat. It is so steep and stony as to make circulation impossible; one's only course is to plant a camp chair among the stones or to look for a soft spot in the pebbles, and to abide in the position so chosen; and yet it is the spot in Étretat most sacred to tranquil pleasure.

The French do not treat their beaches as we do ours —as places for a glance, a dip, or a trot, places animated simply during the couple of hours of bathing time and wrapped in natural desolation for the rest of the twenty-four. They love them, they adore them, they take possession of them, they encamp upon them. The people here sit upon the beach from morning till night; whole families come early and establish themselves, with umbrellas and rugs, books and work. The ladies get sunburnt and don't mind it; the gentlemen smoke interminably; the children roll over on the pointed pebbles and stare at the sun like young eagles. (The children's lot I rather commiserate; they have no wooden spades and pails; they have no sand to delve and grub in; they can dig no trenches and canals nor see the creeping tide flood them.) The great occupation and amusement is the bathing, which has many entertaining features (I allude to it as a spectacle), especially for strangers, who keep an eye upon national idiosyncrasies. The French take their bathing very seriously; supplemented by *opéra-bouffe* in the evening at the Casino, it quite fills out their lives. The spectators and the bathers commingle in graceful promiscuity; it is the freedom of the golden age. The whole beach seems to be a large family party, in a family which should have radical views as regards some prudish prejudices. There is more or less costume, but the minimum rather than the maximum is found to prevail. Bathers come out of their dressing houses wrapped in short white sheets, which they deposit on the stones; and thus they take an air bath for some minutes, before entering the water. Like everything in France, the bathing is excellently managed, and you feel the firm hand of a paternal and overlooking government the moment you issue from your hut. The government will on no consideration consent to letting you get drowned. There are six or eight worthy old sons of Neptune on the beach—perfect amphibious creatures—who, if you are a newcomer, immediately accost you and demand pledges that you know how to swim. If you do not, they give you much excellent advice, guide your infant steps, and keep an eye on you while you are in the water. They are, moreover, obliged to render you any service you may demand—to pour buckets of water over your head, to fetch your bathing sheet and your slippers, to carry your wife and children into the sea, to dip them, cheer and sustain them, to teach them how to swim and how to dive, to hover about, in short, like trickling Providences. At a short distance from the shore are two boats, freighted with more of these marine divinities, who remain there perpetually, and take it as a personal offense if you catch a cramp or venture out too far.

There has, I believe, never been a life lost in bathing at Étretat, and this fair record is a part of the fortune of the town. I see no reason why it should ever be tarnished, however, for the French are noticeably good swimmers. Everyone swims, and swims well—men, women, and children. I have been especially struck with the prowess of the ladies, who take the neatest possible headers from the two long plunging boards which are rigged in the water upon high wheels. As you recline upon the beach, you may observe Mlle. X.[4] issue from her cabin—Mlle. X., the actress of the Palais Royal Theater, whom you have seen and applauded behind the footlights. She wears a bathing dress in which, as regards the trousers, even what I have called the minimum has been appreciably scanted; but she trips down, surveying her breezy nether limbs. *"C'est convenable, j'espère, eh?"* says Mademoiselle, and trots up the springboard which projects over the waves with one end uppermost, like a great seesaw. She balances a moment, and then gives a great aerial dive, executing on the way the most graceful of somersaults. This performance Mlle. X. repeats during the ensuing hour, at intervals of five minutes, and leaves you, as you lie tossing little stones into the water, to ponder the curious and delicate question why a lady may go so far as to put herself into a single scant, clinging garment and take a straight leap, head downward, before 300 spectators, without violation of propriety— leaving the impropriety to begin with her turning over in the air in such a way that for five seconds her head is upward. The logic of the matter is mysterious; white and black are divided by a hair. But the fact remains that virtue is on one side of the hair and vice on the other. There are some days here so still and radiant, however, that it seems as if vice itself, steeped in such an air and such a sea, might be diluted into innocence. The sea is as blue as melted sapphires, and the ragged white faces of the bordering cliffs look like a setting of silver. Everyone is idle, amused, good-natured; the bathers take the water as easily as mermen and mermaids. The bathing men in the two *bateaux de surveillance* have taken aboard a freight of rosy children, more or less chubbily naked, and they have nailed a gay streamer and a rude nosegay to their low mastheads. The swimmers dip and rise, circling round the boats and playing with the children. Every now and then they grasp the sides of the boats and cling to them in a dozen harmonious attitudes, making one fancy that Eugène Delacroix's great picture of Dante and Virgil on the Styx, with the damned trying to scramble into Charon's bark, has been repainted as a scene on one of the streams of Paradise. The swimmers are not the damned, but the blessed, and the demonstrative French babies are the cherubs. The Casino at Étretat is a modest but respectable institution, with a sufficiently capacious terrace, directly upon the beach, a café, a billiard room, a ballroom—which may also be used as a theater, a reading room, and a *salon de conversation*. It is in very good taste, without any attempt at gilding or mirrors; the ballroom, in fact, is quite a masterpiece, with its charm of effect produced simply by unpainted woods and happy proportions.

Three evenings in the week a bland young man in a white cravat plays waltzes on a grand piano; but the effect is not that of an American "hop," owing to the young ladies of France not being permitted to dance in public places. They may only sit wistfully beside their mammas. Imagine a "hop" at which sweet seventeen is condemned to immobility. The burden of the gaiety is sustained by three or four robust English maidens and as many lighter-footed Americans. On the other evenings a weak little operatic troupe gives light specimens of the lyric drama, the privilege of enjoying which is covered by one's subscription to the Casino. The French hurry in joyously (four times a week in July and August!) at the sound of the bell, but I can give no report of the performances. Sometimes I look through the lighted windows and see, on the diminutive stage, a short-skirted young woman with one hand on her heart and the other persuasively extended. Through the hot, unpleasant air comes a little ghost of a roulade. I turn away and walk on the terrace and listen to the ocean vocalizing to the stars. But there are (by daylight) other walks at Étretat than the terrace, and no account of the place is complete without some commemoration of the superb cliffs. They are the finest I have seen; their fantastic needles and buttresses, at either end of the little bay, give to Étretat a striking individuality. Their height is magnificent; if a poor eye for measurement is to be trusted, I should say it was, on an average, an affair of 200 feet. In spite of there being no sands, a persistent admirer of nature will walk a long distance upon the tiresome sea margin of pebbles for the sake of being under them and visiting some of their quiet caves and shadowed corners. Seen thus from directly below, they look stupendous; they rise up like certain great mountain walls in the Alps. They are marvelously white and straight and smooth; they have the tone and something of the surface of time-yellowed marble, and here and there, at their summits, they break into quaint little pinnacles and turrets. But to be on the top of them is even better; here you may walk over miles of grassy, breezy down, with the woods, contorted and sea-stunted, of old farmsteads on your land side (the farmhouses here have all a charming way of being buried in a wood, like the castle of the Sleeping Beauty), coming every little while upon a weather-blackened old shepherd and his flock (their conversation—the shepherds'—is delightful), or on some little seaward-plunging valley, holding in its green hollow a diminutive agricultural village, curtained round from the sea winds by a dense circular stockade of trees. So you may go southward or northward without impediment to Havre or to Dieppe.

HENRY JAMES, JR.
August 26, 1876

APPENDIX

DOCUMENTS RELATING TO HENRY JAMES'S ASSOCIATION
WITH THE NEW YORK "TRIBUNE" INCLUDING HIS COR-
RESPONDENCE WITH WHITELAW REID

The James-Reid correspondence used in this volume
is to be found in the archives of the *Tribune* (now the
New York *Herald Tribune*) where it is filed in Letter
Books chronologically arranged. Reid's letters are exact
reproductions made by a process which transferred the
original script to sheets of a tissue-like paper. Owing
to the smallness of the handwriting, the kind of paper
used for duplicating, and the blurring caused by the
process itself, Reid's letters are not entirely legible.
James's letters are holograph and may be read without
difficulty. Other pieces of correspondence have been
included here to provide a complete documentary picture. With the exception of the very first letter in the
sequence, which is taken from Royal Cortissoz, *The
Life of Whitelaw Reid* (New York, 1921), the items
have been copied from the *Tribune* Letter Books.

[JOHN HAY TO WHITELAW REID, JULY 24, 1875.]

Henry James, Jr., wants to write for the *Tribune*,
letters from Paris, where he is going to live for some

· *209* ·

time to come. He considers the *Tribune* the only paper where business could be combined with literary ambition. I hope you will engage him instead of Houssaye. He will write better letters than anybody—you know his wonderful style and keen observation of life and character. He has no hesitation in saying that he can beat Houssaye on his own ground, gossip and chronicle, and I agree with him. Besides, his name is almost, if not quite, equally valuable—and far more regarded by cultivated people. He would cost not more than half what Houssaye costs (counting translation) and I think his letters would be about twice as good. He would not interfere with Huntington but would simply take Houssaye's place—and in my opinion fill it much better.

He will start in the autumn some time. You might let Houssaye run on until James gets there and then discharge him with a Grantish letter telling him how delighted you and the public have been with his letters, but that the labor of translation has been very difficult and now has become almost impossible through the removal from New York of the invaluable roster who did it, etc., etc.

In short, this is the statement. You pay Houssaye $30 for a not very good letter and me, Heaven knows how much for translating it. For, say, $20 or $25 James will write you a much better letter and sign his name to it.

His address is 20 Quincy St., Cambridge, Mass. You can write to him or to me.

Appendix

My dear Hay:

I agree with you about Houssaye more fully probably than you expected. My plan about him, as I think I mentioned to you [word illegible], was to let him run on 5 or 6 weeks and then, unless he [wore?] well, look up some other novelty. Only the other day we were saying that it was [now?] enough to keep up Houssaye, like John Paul and other light matter, through the summer, but that in the autumn or winter we should have to make a change.

I think exceedingly well of Henry James, though in view of Huntington I doubt whether it is desirable to pay him more than $20 a letter. [We? He?] should want to use his signature, I think [or?] his initial and identify them at the [end?].

If you like pray go ahead and make the bargain with him. I should not, however, make it for any fixed length of time. The [*Tribune* constituency?] loves a change now and then except in the case of a few men like Smalley who are perennial favorites. . . .

Faithfully yours,
WHITELAW REID

[MEMORANDUM BY WHITELAW REID, AUGUST 11, 1875.]

Henry James Jr. is engaged to do Paris letters in place of Houssaye at $20 gold, per letter, to begin about 25th October, 1875.

W. R.

[HENRY JAMES TO WHITELAW REID, FROM PARIS, 29 RUE DE LUXEMBOURG, NOVEMBER 22, 1875.]

My dear Sir:

I enclose herewith my first attempt at a letter to the *Tribune*. I hope it will pass muster. I have been here but a few days and feel by no means *au courant* or wound up to the writing pitch. This is a thing which will have to come little by little; the lapse of time will help me more and more to do as I desire. Meanwhile I will do what I can. I have unfortunately had no *Tribune* at hand, and have not been able to take a very accurate measure of my copy. I am afraid there will be rather too much than too little. I hope, however, that there will be about just enough. Let me also hope that any heading prefixed to the letter will be as brief and simple as possible. The above is my permanent address. I beg you, if Mr. Hay is in New York, to commend me very kindly to him.

Yours very truly
HENRY JAMES JR.

Appendix

[EXCERPT FROM A LETTER FROM WHITELAW REID TO GEORGE W. SMALLEY, LONDON CORRESPONDENT OF THE "TRIBUNE" AND CONTINENTAL CHIEF OF "TRIBUNE" CORRESPONDENTS, JANUARY 15, 1876.]

Probably your inquiry about Paris correspondence may need a word of explanation. My understanding was that you were to undertake to furnish a good weekly letter from Paris, securing some correspondent who was satisfactory both to you and ourselves, and any arrangement we might make with Henry James would be wholly outside of that. The regular Paris correspondent [would?] deal with politics, news, [whatsoever?] may be appropriate. James's letters would be, like Houssaye's, things apart. The same with Trollope. We may or may not continue him, but he is, of course, outside the arrangement made with you. . . .

[WHITELAW REID TO HENRY JAMES, MARCH 27, 1876.]

Dear Sir:

I have yours of the 11th inst. enclosing your tenth letter to the *Tribune* and asking payment for that number. Our representative in London, Mr. Geo. W. Smalley, 15 Pall Mall, will on receipt of this forward you the amount.

I assume that your plans are not likely to take you much away from Paris for some months to come. If I am wrong in this I should be glad to be advised early. Some applications have been made for Parisian correspondence, which we have denied at once, preparing to have the benefit of your services as long as we can.

The letters have not made much [talk?] in the newspapers, but I think they have given a great deal of satisfaction to a large majority of our readers. Houssaye continues to work a little and is anxious to have [say?] a letter a month.

You will be sorry to hear that [John Hay?] is not quite so well as usual, and in consequence is not giving us as much work as we would like. His wife [several words illegible] this week, but returns within a few days. I fancy that their European trip for this summer is practically abandoned, although they have hardly brought themselves to admit it yet.

Very truly yours,

WHITELAW REID

[HENRY JAMES TO WHITELAW REID, 29 RUE DE LUXEMBOURG, PARIS, APRIL 11, 1876.]

My dear Sir:

I receive your letter just as I am about to enclose another missive to the *Tribune*. Many thanks for the order upon Mr. Smalley, which I will today forward to him.

I am glad you have reason to believe that my letters are pleasing to most of your readers—that they could find an echo in the other papers I never expected. I am quite contented with such publicity as the *Tribune* gives them. I am likely (from present appearances) to be in Paris for an indefinite period to come. I shall go away for the summer (after July 1) but I shall remain in France, and be able to write, I hope, two or three times a month. In the autumn I shall almost to a certainty be back here for next winter. You may therefore continue to count upon me.

Many thanks for your news about Hay, which I am sorry is not better. I hope strongly that his bad health is a very temporary annoyance. Will you give him (and to Mrs. Hay) my kind regards and the assurance of my sympathy? I regret that I am not to have the pleasure of seeing them this summer.

Yours very truly

HENRY JAMES JR.

[HENRY JAMES TO WHITELAW REID, PARIS, 29 RUE DE LUXEMBOURG, APRIL 23, 1876.]

My dear Mr. Reid:

I enclose another—a 14th letter. Let me add a most earnest and urgent request that the practice of inserting headings to the successive paragraphs in my letters, which I see was begun on April 1 last, be not continued. I object to it in the strongest possible manner and I entreat and beseech you to cause it to be sup-

pressed. May I not safely count on your doing so? The
thing is in every way disagreeable to me.

Yours very truly

HENRY JAMES JR.

Memorandum written on the back of the preceding
letter to Whitelaw Reid by a member of his staff. (The
James dispatch referred to is that of April 1, 1876,
"Parisian Topics.")

The letter of April 1, being a very long one, Mr. Ford
put crossheads in it. We have not used them since, and
will not unless you say so especially.

O'Dwyer.

[HENRY JAMES TO WHITELAW REID, ÉTRETAT, JULY 25, 1876.]

My dear Mr. Reid:

I send the *Tribune* another letter, after a longer interval than usual, occasioned by a dearth of topics during the last two or three weeks of my stay in Paris. I
am here at a curious little sea-bathing place, to which,
a few days hence, I will devote a letter. I must leave
your people the responsibility of baptising the one I
enclose. It is chiefly about Rouen.

I applied to Mr. Smalley some days ago for payment for the letters I had sent you (with the exception
of one, the 19th—) since the receipt of the check you

authorized him to send me for eight letters, though, as he said, the proceeding was irregular, he not being authorized afresh. The next time I will apply to you directly.

I should like to propose you—on this point—an augmentation; viz.: that, beginning with the letter I enclose, I receive *thirty dollars* per letter. Will you be so good as to let me know whether this is agreeable to you?

Very truly yours
HENRY JAMES JR.

[WHITELAW REID TO HENRY JAMES, AUGUST 10, 1876.]

Dear Mr. James:

I am in receipt of your favor of the 25th July suggesting an advance of one-half the payment for your letters.

I have been on the point of writing you making a suggestion of a quite different nature. It was to the effect that the letters should be made rather more "newsy" in character, and somewhat shorter, and that they should be sent somewhat less frequently. The reason [is that we are?] approaching the most interesting period of the Centennial Exhibition, and are just entering the active part of the Presidential campaign. At this time we have less room for foreign matters, and find less interest among our readers for what foreign correspondence we do get room to print.

In addition to this we have feared that your letters were sometimes on topics too remote from popular interests to please more than a select few of our readers. The *Tribune* constituency is undoubtedly the most intelligent one possessed by any of the widely circulated newspapers, but it is certainly possible to overestimate its literary culture and interest in the [pure?] literary treatment of a subject. We must not forget that the people who read newspapers are often hurried and nearly always [we find?] that they like brevity, variety, and topics of wide interest—that they are much more likely to read a one-column letter than one of two columns, and that even when the limit is fixed at a column it is best, as the candid churchgoer said to his parson, to err on the side of mercy.

If you can adopt this suggestion, I think you will agree with me that there would then be less occasion for a change in the rate of payment.

You must not imagine that any of us have failed to appreciate the admirable work you have done for us. The difficulty has sometimes been not that it was too good, but that it was magazine rather than newspaper work.

Very truly yours,

WHITELAW REID

[HENRY JAMES TO WHITELAW REID, CHÂTEAU DE VARENNES (NEAR MONTARGIS), AUGUST 30, 1876.]

Dear Mr. Reid:

I have just received your letter of August 10th. I quite appreciate what you say about the character of my letters, and about their not being the right sort of thing for a newspaper. I have been half expecting to hear from you to that effect. I myself had wondered whether you could make room for them during the present and coming time at home, and I can easily imagine that the general reader should feel indisposed to give the time requisite for reading them. They would, as you say, be more in place in a magazine. But I am afraid I can't assent to your proposal that I should try and write otherwise. I know the sort of letter you mean —it is doubtless the proper sort of thing for the *Tribune* to have. But I can't produce it—I don't know how and I couldn't learn how. It would cost me really more trouble than to write as I have been doing (which comes tolerably easy to me) and it would be poor economy for me to try and become "newsy" and gossipy. I am too finical a writer and I should be constantly becoming more "literary" than is desirable. To resist this tendency would be rowing upstream and would take much time and pains. If my letters have been "too good" I am honestly afraid that they are the poorest I can do, especially for the money! I had better, therefore, suspend them altogether. I have enjoyed writing them, however, and if the *Tribune* has not been the better for them I hope it has not been too much the worse. I shall doubtless have sooner or later a discreet successor. Believe me, with the best wishes,

Yours very truly
HENRY JAMES JR.

[HENRY JAMES TO WHITELAW REID, 3 BOLTON STREET, PICCA-DILLY, DECEMBER 21, 1876.]

My dear Mr. Reid:

I have just received your draft upon Paris for three hundred francs, for which I am much obliged and which it has been no inconvenience to wait for.

—I have transferred myself, you will see by my date, to London, whence I sometimes wish there were an occasional pretext for writing to the *Tribune*. But with Mr. Smalley here there of course can be none whatever. I have seen him and he has been very kind to me.

Yours very truly
HENRY JAMES JR.

[MEMORANDUM ON BACK OF PRECEDING LETTER.]

Whitelaw Reid to his secretary: Miss Hutchinson: Do you think he can do a clever piece of work for us now and then? W. R.

Reply: Mr. Reid: I don't know how to form a judgment about this. Excuse me. M. H.

[WHITELAW REID TO HENRY JAMES, JANUARY 16, 1877.]

Dear Mr. James:

I wish I saw how I could avail myself of the information contained in your pleasant note of 21st December, by asking you for a hand on letters now and then on some particular point. The truth is, however, that our Mr. Smalley covers the field fully and furnishes so much copy that we find it pretty hard to make room for our other correspondence.

Still don't forget the *Tribune* if you have a chance to do something in our line.

I have ventured to [become?] a little personal about your movements, which I hope will not [touch?] too far upon your private life, or seem disagreeable.

Very truly yours,

WHITELAW REID

[HENRY JAMES TO WHITELAW REID, 3 BOLTON STREET, PICCADILLY, W., FEBRUARY 2, 1877.]

My dear Mr. Reid:

Your note of January 16th came to me a couple of days since. My allusion to occasionally sending you something from London was merely *pro forma;* I know too well how little, both in quantity and quality, in the way of correspondence Mr. Smalley leaves to be desired. I am very well occupied and shall probably not soon (in London, at least) feel justified in sending you anything—save my good wishes.—I have not seen the paragraph (personal) to which you allude; but I think I can rest in the confidence that it does me no undue violence.

Yours very truly
H. JAMES JR.

[HENRY JAMES TO WHITELAW REID, NEW YORK, 115 EAST 25TH ST., SUNDAY P.M. [18 DECEMBER 1881?]]

Dear Mr. Reid:

I have delayed writing to you till this evening in answer to your friendly note, in order that I might be a little more clear in mind as to the number of days to which my present stay in New York is to extend. I hope very much my delay has not brought you inconvenience—especially as I am obliged to say to you that I am afraid I shall be leaving town (for Christmas) too soon to have the pleasure of dining with you. My present plan is to go on Thursday next to Cambridge, to spend the festival just mentioned, at my father's, and remain there for several days. How long I shall be in New York on my return (as I am going to Washington) I don't know as yet; but if it should be for an appreciable time it will give me great pleasure to let you know, and name a day, as you propose. I don't propose one before that, as I am dining out continuously until Thursday evening inclusive— and am very sorry to be able just now to do so little honour to your hospitality. But I shall not fail later, if the occasion comes. Meanwhile I send kind regards to Mrs. Reid, and remain with many thanks very truly yours

H. JAMES

[HENRY JAMES TO WHITELAW REID, 20 QUINCY STREET, CAMBRIDGE, MASS., DEC. 26TH [1881].]

Dear Mr. Reid:

I am *sure*, just now, of being in New York only on Saturday and Sunday next—or I should perhaps say of being there disengaged, for I return thither from this place on Wednesday. On Saturday or Sunday I shall be very happy to dine with you, and if you will send me a word (to 115 East 25th St.) saying which of these days (if either is open to you) you prefer, I will hold the engagement sacred. I am not to be at Godkins (who has gone, till Monday next, to Cincinnati) but don't know at what hotel I shall be able to lodge. I owe you as usual an apology for delay— caused also as usual by my uncertainty from day to day as to my comings, goings, and stayings. With all the good wishes of the season to yourself and Mrs. Reid, believe me very truly yours

H. JAMES

[HENRY JAMES TO WHITELAW REID, NEW YORK, 115 EAST 25TH STREET, DECEMBER 29, 1881.]

Dear Mr. Reid:

I this moment find your note, and will with pleasure present myself on Saturday at seven. With kind regards,

Very truly yours
H. JAMES

[HENRY JAMES TO WHITELAW REID, BOSTON, 131 MT. VERNON ST., JULY 22, 1883.]

Dear Mr. Reid:

I wonder if it would be in your power to direct a slight service to be performed for my advantage? If this is the case I shall be very grateful.

Several years ago—in the winter, spring, and summer of 1876—I wrote from Paris certain letters—some dozen in all, I suppose, to the *Tribune*. The question has come up of my collecting into a volume various sketches of travel that I have produced during the last ten years; and it occurs to me that in this collection portions of those letters may be adapted to figure. But I haven't the articles themselves—they are buried, so far as I have kept them, in the interstices of a heap of luggage that I have stowed away in Europe. Might this appeal to you have the result of supplying the void? In other words, are the back numbers of the *Tribune*, as far back as 1876, preserved at the office, and would it be in your power to ask one of your myrmidons to search among them for those that contain my letters? I don't want all of them, but as I am unable to specify, it would be well, I am afraid, that all of them should, if possible, be sent. They are comprised within the said year 1876, and are in almost all cases, I think, surmounted with my name. For any trouble connected with this undertaking I should be much your debtor, even if it should not prove wholly fruitful. I have been in America these seven months, but only a few days in New York or I should have seen you. I have been detained in this place, and am still detained by family affairs. I beg to be kindly recalled to Mrs. Reid, and am very truly yours

HENRY JAMES

[HENRY JAMES TO WHITELAW REID, BOSTON, MOUNT VERNON ST., JULY 27, 1883.]

Dear Mr. Reid:

I thank you kindly for your note of the 24th in regard to my old letters in the *Tribune* and for the information you caused to be collected for me on the subject. This information is valuable and helps to solve my difficulty. You are so good as to say that it would be in your power to have such of the letters as I should wish, copied for me in the office. I shall take the liberty of profiting by this offer and asking you to please direct three of them to be transcribed—the only ones I desire. When the copies are sent me, be so good as to order that a note of the cost be sent with them that I may transmit to the office the sum. I subjoin the three dates and remain

Very truly yours

HENRY JAMES

Tribune, 1876: April 29, August 12, 26.

To the copyist. Please leave a considerable margin.

[HENRY JAMES TO WHITELAW REID, NEWPORT, R. I., AUGUST 8, 1883.]

Dear Mr. Reid:

Your note of the 1st was last night forwarded to me from Boston, having been kept there for some days, with many other letters, while I was moving from one place to another. It was accompanied by the three letters from the *Tribune*, in the original text and most neatly and conveniently arranged. I thank you extremely for the attention you have given to my request, and I am especially indebted to the ingenious young Drury, whose researches were so brilliantly conducted. Will you please cause him to be assured of my thanks and direct that the enclosed note ($5.00) be delivered to him for his trouble in looking up the papers? I hope you are not personally in New York, in this fine summer weather, as much as you are officially.

Very faithfully yours
HENRY JAMES

NOTES

LETTER 1

[1] Marie Céline Chaumont (1848(?)–1926) began her stage career at eleven at the Théâtre Molière. She appeared first in comedies, playing the child's role in *L'Ami des Femmes* by Dumas *fils* in 1864 at the Gymnase. In 1869 she gave up comedy for operetta at the Bouffes-Parisiens.

[2] The old Paris Opera had been destroyed by fire. The new building—the one seen by visitors to Paris today—was opened on January 5, 1865. Its architect, Jean-Joseph Garnier (also designer of the casino of Monte Carlo), had labored for fourteen years on the edifice.

[3] James is referring to the panic of 1873, precipitated by the failure of Jay Cooke, financier of the Northern Pacific Railroad. It lasted five years and brought drastic mercantile losses.

[4] During 1871–1875, the steps leading toward the adoption of constitutional laws establishing the form of republican government in France were of extreme national and international importance, for they determined the future of modern France. The Third Republic (which lasted until the German invasion of France in World War II) had been officially proclaimed in 1870, following the collapse of the government of Napoleon III. For several years it had functioned without a constitution, but now the groundwork for permanent government was being laid.

[5] Alexandre Dumas *fils* (1824–1895), natural son of Alexandre Dumas *père* (1803–1870), achieved fame with *La Dame aux Camélias* (1852), one of the great stage successes of the second half of the nineteenth century. His subsequent

plays (including *L'Étrangère*) espoused conventional morality. The psychological orientation of Dumas' work, reflecting an unhappy childhood spent in the demimonde atmosphere frequented by his father, was alien to James, who often criticized Dumas' choice of subject matter.

[6] The order of the six leading Parisian newspapers in point of circulation, as estimated in 1858, was: *Siècle, Presse, Constitutionnel, Patrie, Débats,* and *Assemblée.* In 1878 the total number of journals of all kinds published in France was 2,200. *Le Figaro* had a circulation of about 70,000.

[7] Victorien Sardou (1831–1908) came into prominence about 1860, with a succession of satirical comedies. Later he turned to historical melodramas, many written for Sarah Bernhardt. He was elected to the French Academy in 1878. Highly prolific, he was for James a symbol of artistic cleverness in the invidious sense of the word. *Ferréol* was produced at the Gymnase Theater on December 17, 1875.

[8] Ambroise Thomas (1811–1896). His *Hamlet* was first produced at the Opera on March 9, 1868. The title role was originally cast for a tenor, but the Opera had no one capable of creating the part. Thomas, accordingly, changed the music to suit a baritone and Jean-Baptiste Faure (1830–1914) achieved great renown in the role. Mme. Carvalho (Marie Miolan), soprano, who played the female lead, was known for her grace and finish.

[9] Luca Giordano (1632–1705) painted the ceiling decoration in the Palazzo Medici.

[10] Paul Baudry (1828–1886). His decorations of the Grand Opera are regarded as his greatest work. The scheme comprises thirty-three large separate compositions. In size and completeness it was the most important decorative enterprise carried out by one man since the great days of the Renaissance.

[11] Ernesto Rossi (1827–1896) was the first Italian actor to play Shakespeare's *Othello* (in 1856) before Paris audi-

ences. He was much admired in France and Germany. His style of acting was never acceptable in England or America and James's doubts about Rossi's reception in the United States proved accurate.

[12] Frédéric Lemaître (1800–1876). His power and brilliance were legendary, and his performance in the title role of *Kean* was still within memory.

LETTER 2

[1] Louis Barye (1796–1875) was exceptionally popular in America, more so, even, than in France. The Walters Museum at Baltimore kept a specimen (received from Barye himself) of every work he produced; the Corcoran Gallery at Washington had a full collection, and the chief contribution for a posthumous exhibition and monument to Barye came from American supporters. James's designation of a liking for Barye's work as the sign of "not . . . a refined, but at least an enterprising taste," offended some of Barye's admirers and a letter protesting James's harsh judgment of the animal miniatures was published in the *Tribune* January 22, 1876. Barye seems to have been a model for James's "cats and monkeys" man in "The Madonna of the Future," the vulgar artist whose "expressive little brutes" were "revolting" in their "imitative felicity."

[2] Jean-Baptiste Carpeaux (1827–1875). Carpeaux's group, "La Danse," created such a furor when first installed in the Opera house that it was ordered removed. Attempted mutilation of the group by incensed Parisians and the death of Carpeaux, which followed shortly thereafter, caused a shift in public opinion out of respect for the sculptor, and the work was left standing. The objections to it were on the grounds of its realism. James's description of "poor, lean

individual bodies . . . pitifully real," resembling "the undressed lady and gentleman . . . as distinguished from the
unconsciously naked heroes and heroines of Greek art," reveals him to be almost as uncomfortable in the presence of
Carpeaux's figures as the French at first were.

³ The Odéon Theater opened originally on May 20, 1797.
It frequently changed its name, being the Théâtre de l'Im-
pératrice from 1805–1815, the Théâtre Royal under three
kings, the Impérial, under Napoleon III, and today again the
Odéon and the second national theater. The present building
opened in 1819.

⁴ The bust of Voltaire in the Théâtre Français was by Jean-
Antoine Houdon (1741–1828); the pieces on exhibition in the
redecorated Odéon Theater were by Émile-Auguste Carolus-
Duran (1838–1917); Alexander Schoenewerk (1820–1885);
Henri Chapu (1833–1891); and Albert-Ernest Carrier de
Belleuse—who signed himself Carrier—(1824–1887).

⁵ Pauline Virginie Déjazet (1797–1875) first appeared as
a child actress and played in Paris and in the provinces. From
1831 she was chiefly associated with the Palais Royal.

LETTER 3

¹ The election of the permanent senators marked the beginning of a republican majority in the chamber. President
MacMahon had been chosen by the monarchical Right; thus
the "victory of the Left" (of the republicans) in the election
was indeed "dramatic." It forced MacMahon to follow a republican policy and to select a ministry from the Left Center.

² Hippolyte Taine (1828–1893), the French critic and historian, became famous with his *Revue de l'Instruction Pu-
blique* (1855–1856), a series of articles attacking the French
philosophers of the early 19th century and setting forth a

system in which the methods of the exact sciences were applied to psychological and metaphysical research. In 1864 Taine was made professor at the École des Beaux Arts, a position which he held for twenty years. His *Histoire de la Littérature Anglaise,* in which his deterministic views were set forth in uncompromising fashion, appeared in 1863. Shocked by the French disasters of 1870–1871, he started to apply his analytical methods to the history of his own country. The first volume of *Les Origines de la France Contemporaine,* begun in 1871, was therefore eagerly awaited. James's dismissal of Taine's philosophic ideas is an interesting reflection of his American intellectual orientation. *Les Origines* has often been admired for its vigor of style, but from the French point of view its importance was ideological; it confronted the public with a criticism of the philosophical abstractions upon which the men of the eighteenth century had built their society and which were still widely current. James had reviewed Taine's work four times previously, in the *Nation* and the *Atlantic Monthly.*

LETTER 4

[1] Ernest Meissonier (1815–1891) won great acclaim the world over for his early genre paintings, characterized by their incredible minuteness of detail. Meissonier was extremely nearsighted and his inability to visualize objects at a distance probably explains his notable lack of success in large historical canvases. "1807," which ultimately found a home at the Metropolitan Museum, is judged by critics as among the poorest of Meissonier's efforts in this line.

[2] Alexander Stewart (1803–1876) was an American merchant who founded the drygoods business which gradually became one of the largest mercantile organizations in the world. He was at one time considered the wealthiest man in

the United States and attracted much attention by the lavishness of his donations to charitable institutions and his expenditures for *objets d'art.*

³ Sir Richard Wallace (1818–1890) was the English connoisseur whose great collection is now housed in Hertford House, London. During the years 1873–1885 he lived mostly in Paris.

⁴ James's recollection of the date of the battle of Eylau is correct: it was fought in the snow on February 8, 1807.

Letter 5

¹ The famous actors named here are: François Joseph Talma (1763–1826); Anne Françoise Hippolyte (Mlle. Mars) (1787–1867); Marie Thomas Amélie Delaunay (Mlle. Dorval) (1798–1849); Élisa Félix (Rachel) (1820–1858); and Antoine Louis Prosper (Frédéric Lemaître) (1800–1876).

² Rose Chéri (1824–1861) played many parts in the plays of Augier and Dumas *fils,* chiefly at the Gymnase. Aimée Olympe Desclée (1836–1874) also won fame through Dumas *fils,* playing the lead in *Frou-Frou.* She was particularly good as the heroine in *Visite de Noces* (1871) and *La Femme de Claude* (1873). She died suddenly, at the height of her success, in 1874. James saw her during his boyhood when the James family resided for a time in Paris. See James's *A Small Boy and Others* (1913), Chapter XXVI.

³ Henry Irving's production of *Macbeth* took place at the Lyceum on September 18, 1875. Charles Kemble (1775–1854), who first played in *Macbeth* as Malcolm at seventeen, was regarded as more suited for poetic drama than for tragedy, excelling in such roles as Mercutio, Benedick, and Romeo. Edmund Kean (1787–1833) was noted for his strong imaginative appeal in parts which had a touch of malign or murderous frenzy—Shylock, Iago, Othello, and Macbeth, all

of which he rendered with a passion verging on extravagance.

⁴ Jacques Offenbach (1819–1880) composed sixty-five operettas in twenty-five years, of which the most popular, during the period of James's stay in Paris, were *La Vie Parisi-
enne* (1866), *Barbe Bleue* (1866), and *La Grande Duchesse
de Gerolstein* (1867). Alexandre Lecocq (1832–1918), also
prolific, was most successful with *La Fille de Madame Angot*
(1873), which was performed 400 nights consecutively.
Among the numerous hits of Hervé (Florimond Rongé)
(1825–1892) the most popular was *l'Oeuil Crevé.*

⁵ In *La Cruche Cassée,* a comic opera by Noirac and
Moineaux, with music by Vasseur, Céline Chaumont played
the part of Colette.

⁶ Anna Marie Louise Judic (1849–1911) joined the Bouffes-
Parisiens in 1872 and soon became the leading lady of *opéra
bouffe.* In *La Créole,* a comic opera with music by Jacques
Offenbach, she played the part of Zoë.

⁷ James evidently enjoyed Rossi more as Kean than as Macbeth. (See Letter 1.)

⁸ Gustave Hippolyte Worms (1837–1910) began his career
at the Théâtre Français, where he remained for seven years.
He then went to Russia for ten years and on his return in
1875 was a great success at the Gymnase. Émile Zola shared
James's enthusiasm for Worms, especially admiring his im-
position of realism upon romanticism in his acting technique.

⁹ Louis-Arsène Delaunay (1826–1903) was a seasoned
actor, having first appeared at the Odéon in 1846. From 1848
he had been with the Théâtre Français.

¹⁰ *Petite Pluie,* a comedy by Edmond Pailleron, was first
produced at the Théâtre Français December 4, 1875.

¹¹ Jeanne Arnould-Plessy (1819–1897) first appeared at
the Théâtre Français in 1834 and became a *sociétaire* within
the year. In 1845 she left Paris to marry J. F. Arnould, a
dramatist, in London. For ten years she played with brilliant
success in St. Petersburg. She returned to the Théâtre Fran-

çais in 1855 (as a *pensionnaire*). Her farewell performance took place on May 8, 1876.

[12] The Variétés was first opened in 1807. The present building bearing this name is situated at 7, Boulevard Montmartre. The original Palais Royal opened in 1831; in 1848 it became the Théâtre de Montansier, reverting to the name of Palais Royal in 1852. It was almost completely rebuilt in 1881.

[13] *Le Panache* was a comedy in three acts by Edmond Gondinet, first produced at the Palais Royal Theater on October 12, 1875.

[14] *Les Scandales d'Hier,* a comedy in three acts by Théodore Barrière, was first produced at the Vaudeville Theater, Paris, on November 15, 1875, with Blanche Pierson (1842–1919) and Pierre Berton (1843–1912) in the cast.

Letter 6

[1] In the first general elections held under the new constitution in February 1876, the Republican party, hitherto united under the leadership of Gambetta in a common front against both Royalists and Bonapartists, split into halves. The moderate wing, whose aim was to adopt a political and parliamentary method which consisted in limiting the scope of reforms and avoiding disruptive issues, dissociated itself from the Radicals, the wing that was demanding rapid reforms. The parties on the right consisted of the Royalists, Legitimates, Orleanists, and the Bonapartists. Throughout the formative period of the parliamentary republic, whenever diverse issues split public opinion, this cleavage was reflected in a variety of changed alignments of factions in the multiparty system. Every ministry had to be a coalition of several groups, and being based on only a limited area of agreement, tended

to be short-lived and to collapse as soon as one or two marginal elements deserted it.

[2] Louis (Joseph) Buffet (1818–1898) was president of the Assembly, 1872–1875. He was Minister of the Interior and vice-president of the Council from March 1875 to February 23, 1876.

[3] James gained admittance to several coteries in Paris. His comments on them, therefore, reflect personal experience. He had been taken by Turgenev to Flaubert's Sunday afternoons, where he met Zola, Daudet, Maupassant, and Edmond de Goncourt. In other coteries he was meeting Renan and the French critic, Schérer.

[4] James's reference to "Mr. A. and Mr. X." echoes his exclamation to Thomas Sergeant Perry in a letter on February 3, 1876: "You should hear the tone which these gentlemen take in regard to Cherbuliez and Droz." Gustave Droz, a minor novelist whom James had reviewed sympathetically in 1871 and still admired, was ridiculed mercilessly by the realists of Flaubert's circle.

[5] The Commune was of very recent memory. It had originated in Paris in 1871. Led by a small but active class of professional revolutionaries, it was precipitated by a sense of civic outrage when German troops marched down the Champs Élysées and when it became known that the national assembly had decided to locate in Versailles rather than in Paris. The uprising, which appealed to the traditions of 1793, failed. Thiers's government retook the city and the repression which followed virtually destroyed the revolutionary parties.

[6] Marie Edmé Patrice Maurice de MacMahon (1808–1893). On the resignation of Thiers in 1873, Marshal MacMahon was elected president by an almost unanimous vote. His term of office was set at seven years. The president was more popular in the rural districts of France than in Paris and other large cities, where criticism of Republican ideas found more open expression in the press.

[7] *Les Danicheff,* a comedy in four acts by Pierre Newsky (Petr Corvin de Krukovskoi) and Alexandre Dumas *fils,* was first produced at the Odéon on January 8, 1876.

[8] Ernesto Rossi's Romeo was widely extolled. It was generally regarded as more suited to his talents than the great tragic roles, allowing more opportunity for the expression of his fervor and romanticism.

LETTER 7

[1] Victor Hugo (1802–1885), leader of the French Romantic movement as poet and novelist, first entered political life after the Revolution of 1848. From the beginning he showed himself to be poor in politics, indulging in such bombastic rhetoric that even his fellows in the House of Peers did not take him seriously. When he stood for the presidency of the Republic after 1848, he obtained very few votes. He spent the years 1851–1870 in exile. His re-entry into the political life of his country during his last years (1870–1885) was more as a symbol than as an effective agent. He was at the height of his literary fame, but the idolatry of his worshipers was counterbalanced by a reaction against his bad qualities—his vulgarity, his intellectual thinness, and his blatant egoism. Elected to the Senate, as James notes, he nevertheless took no part in the debates. James had reviewed Hugo's writings previously in the *Nation,* reacting so strongly against Hugo's verbosity that he felt it necessary to admonish himself against undue severity.

[2] *La Timbale d'Argent, opéra bouffe,* words by Jaime and Noriac, music by Vasseur. Played at the Lyceum Theater with Mlle. Aimée in the lead. *La Petite Mariée,* comic opera in three acts by E. Leterrier, music by Lecocq.

[3] Alphonse de Lamartine (1790–1869), poet and politician, was best known for his *Méditations Poétiques* (1820), reflec-

tive poems of a religious and mystical cast. He took an active part in the administration and politics of his country, being for a short time (in 1848) head of the provisional government.

[4] Marie Favart (Pierette Ignace Pingaud) (1833–1908) was engaged at the Théâtre Français, where she became *sociétaire* in 1854.

[5] Jean Mounet-Sully (1841–1916), tragedian, was engaged at the Théâtre Français in 1872, where he won fame in *Andromaque* and *Le Cid*. He became *sociétaire* in 1873. He played leading roles in *l'Étrangère, Hernani, Ruy Blas, Antigone,* and other classical works.

[6] Ernest Legouvé (1807–1903) was the French dramatist who wrote *Médée* (1855), which gave Ristori a notable part and which led to Legouvé's election to the French Academy. In middle and late life (he was almost seventy when James heard him) he devoted his energies largely to lecturing and propagandizing for women's rights and children's education, in both of which movements he was a French pioneer. Legouvé was an advocate of physical training, was well known as a fencer, and was long regarded as one of the best shots in France.

[7] James seems to have had Emerson in mind, among American lecturers, and perhaps his own father, for he heard Emerson at the Music Hall and Henry James Sr. spoke at Cooper Union.

[8] Francisque Sarcey (1828–1889), dramatic critic for the *Temps,* whose criticism James admired, published a number of volumes on the contemporary theater. He favored formal tradition in acting and supremacy of plot in the construction of stage plays. He was a master of the art of informal lecture. James's estimate of ten minutes' preparation for a lecture probably undercalculates the effort given by Sarcey to an art form which he developed on the principles of Cicero's

De Oratore. Sarcey discussed the techniques of his lecture method in *Recollections of Middle Life* (1893).

⁹ James adapted this amusing anecdote in his novel, *The American,* which he was writing at this time. "What sort of a husband can you get for twelve thousand francs?" asks the little copyist Noémie Nioche of the American, Christopher Newman.

¹⁰ Isidore Pils (1813–1875). The biographical data for James's sketch of Pils seem to have been drawn from Becq de Fouquières' *Isidore Alexandrin Augustin Pils, Sa Vie et Son Oeuvre,* Paris, 1876.

¹¹ Horace Vernet (1758–1836), to whom James compares Pils, was best known for his *Triumph of Paulus Aemilius* (1789), especially for his rendering of the horses in that painting. Two of his best-known military pictures are "Battle of Marengo" (1804) and "Morning of Austerlitz" (1808).

¹² (Jean) Hippolyte Flandrin (1809–1864), historical and portrait painter, was noted for the moral perceptiveness of his portrait work; Jean François Millet (1814–1875) was the genre painter whose representations of peasant life were painted with simple, earnest feeling and a comprehension of its pathos such as few painters have ever attained.

¹³ Ferdinand Victor Eugène Delacroix (1799–1863) won his reputation with exhibition of his "Dante and Virgil" in 1822. The early work referred to by James, "Death of Sardanapalus" is usually dated 1827.

LETTER 8

¹ Louis Blanc (1811–1882), publicist and politician, author of *Histoire de la Révolution Française*.

² Désiré Barodet (1823–1906) entered public life in 1870 as an extreme Republican.

Notes

[3] Léon Gambetta (1838–1882), originally a lawyer, became famous in 1868 for his defense of the journalist Delescluze, which he turned into an attack upon the *coup d'état* of 1851. He was first elected to the Assembly in 1869. He rendered heroic service during the crucial years, 1869–1871, and after a brief period of strategic retirement in Spain, returned to France to agitate for the definitive establishment of the Republic. His parliamentary dexterity and eloquence secured the voting of the constitution in February, 1875. To his policy of moderation he gave the name of "opportunism." His anti-clericalism was launched to counteract the political intrigues for the restoration of the temporal power of the Pope.

[4] James brought to the Catholic University issue a typically American point of view. The problem was "peculiarly difficult," as he acknowledged, but it does not appear that James fully understood how much more difficult such a question was in a context of European politics than of American. Historical evidence shows that as the Royalists came to sponsor the cause of the Church more actively, the ultramontane clericals were trusting that restoration of the monarchy would secure them an influence over policy which was denied them by the Republicans. The Church was not only competing in the matter of education, but was trying to make France the defender of papal interests against the new Italian kingdom and against Bismarck's *Kulturkampf* in Germany. The tradition of hostility between Church and republic and the extent of clerical power in France made protraction of the strife for two more decades inevitable. James was thinking both about the ultimate solution of the problem and the immediate politically-involved question.

[5] "Superior instruction" is one of a number of Gallicisms to be found in the *Tribune* letters. James was translating *l'instruction supérieure* literally. Obviously "higher education" would have been more accurate.

[6] James was more intimately acquainted with monarchist than with radical intemperance. To Alice James, on February 22, 1876, he wrote: "I see none but ardent Monarchists and hear everything vile said about the Republic." The evening on which he was in a room into which M. Buffet entered was either during a visit to the salon of the Marquise de Bloqueville or at a reception held by the Duc d'Aumale, which he attended January 25.

[7] Émile de Girardin (1802–1881), French publicist, founder of *La Presse* and *La Liberté*. His most successful *coup* was the purchase of *Le Petit Journal*.

[8] Georges Lachaud (1846–1896), a Bonapartist, defended the Empire in *Essai sur la Dictature* (1875), *L'Empire* (1877), and other writings.

[9] François Jules Edmond Got (1882–1901) entered the Conservatoire in 1841 and gained first prize for comedy in 1843. He appeared at the Théâtre Français in 1844 and became *sociétaire* in 1850. He retired in 1895. The play in which James saw Got, *Maître Patelin,* was an adaptation of the 15th century farce by Roger Allard.

LETTER 9

[1] The exact occasion of this discussion is revealed in an unpublished letter to Alice James, February 22: "I went for an hour to Flaubert's . . . they were talking about the great theatrical event, Alexandre Dumas' *L'Étrangère* . . . they all detest Dumas—very properly, and predict for him a great fiasco before long."

[2] Sarah Bernhardt (Sarah Henriette Rosine) (1845–1923) began her training for the stage at thirteen, and in 1862 made her first appearance at the Théâtre Français. In 1872, at the Français, she triumphed in *King Lear* and *Ruy Blas,* and

shortly thereafter in *Hernani.* She set out on her travels, making her first appearance in London in 1879 in *Phèdre* and in New York in 1880 in *Adrienne Lecouvreur.* James's designation of her as "that very interesting actress" is notable for its lack of enthusiasm. He was always critical of her as being an excessively histrionic personality.

[3] Benoît Constant Coquelin (1841–1909) entered the Théâtre Français in 1860, becoming *sociétaire* in 1864. He remained with the Français until 1886, shortly before beginning a tour of Europe and America. James, who had been a schoolmate of his at Boulogne-sur-Mer in the late 1850's, devoted an article to him in the *Century Magazine.* It was Coquelin who created the part of Cyrano de Bergerac in Rostand's poetic drama. He was one of the actors in France most admired by the novelist.

[4] Sophie Alexandrine Croizette (1848–1901) was born in Russia. She entered the Conservatoire in 1867, studied under Bressant, and won first prize for comedy in 1869. She appeared at the Théâtre Français in 1870 and was elected *sociétaire* in 1873.

[5] Alexandre-Frédéric Febvre (1835–1916) played in several Paris theaters before joining the Théâtre Français in 1866. He became *sociétaire* in 1867 and retired in 1894.

[6] Marie Camargo (1710–1770) was the great French ballerina for whom Lecocq wrote the opera *Camargo* and for whom Petipa staged a ballet, *Camargo* (1872), to music by Minkus. Carlotta Grisi (1821–1899), famous Italian ballerina of the Romantic period, was the creator of the role of Giselle.

Letter 10

[1] John Lemoinne (1815–1892). Besides his writings for various journals (*Journal des Débats, Le Matin*), Lemoinne wrote many critical studies.

[2] Jules Janin (1804–1874), novelist, critic, and journalist, made his chief bid for fame with his collected dramatic criticism from the *Journal des Débats* (1858), under the title, "Histoire de la Littérature Dramatique." He was called in his time "the prince of critics," but James's charge of superficiality has also found its way into the annals: *"Il ne manquait pas d'esprit, et il avait parfois de la délicatesse, de la grâce; mais, en revanche, on ne trouve chez lui aucun principe, ni même aucune suite"* (*Larousse du XXᵉ Siècle*).

[3] The extent to which the French Academy has represented the best literary life is an often-debated question. In the nineteenth century, for example, considerations of various kinds excluded such notables as Proudhon, Comte, Béranger, Stendhal, Balzac, Gautier, Flaubert, Zola, the brothers Goncourt, Maupassant, Daudet, and even such academic writers as Thierry, Michelet, and Quinet.

[4] When James accepted the contract to write the *Tribune* letters, he requested that "any heading prefixed to the letter will be as brief and simple as possible." He said nothing about the use of subheadings for sections of letters, but his aversion to these was equally strong. The practice of breaking James's text with subheads was first begun in this letter. On April 23 James wrote to Whitelaw Reid ". . . a most earnest and urgent request that the practice . . . be not continued. I object to it in the strongest possible manner and I entreat and beseech you to cause it to be suppressed. . . ." His dislike of headlines and large type finds frequent expression in his fiction.

[5] The image of "the cracked vessel and the sound" was to figure in *The Portrait of a Lady* and to be of the essence in *The Golden Bowl*.

[6] Jean Léon Gérôme (1824–1904), history and genre painter, was the pupil of Paul Delaroche and Charles Gleyre. After studying in Italy, he visited Russia and Egypt in search

of new subjects. His range was wide and included many interpretations of ancient history and myth, as well as contemporary themes.

[7] Albert Delpit (1849–1893) was a French playwright, American by birth, whose second drama was the one James saw and described so amusingly. It had been originally performed at the Théâtre Historique in 1873. The play aroused among French critics the same mockery to be found in James's précis—some suggested that Lincoln would never have become known had it not been for his dramatic assassination. Delpit wrote prolifically, as journalist, novelist, poet, and playwright.

[8] Victor Tissot (1845–1917) was a Swiss, educated in Tuebingen and Vienna. He came to Paris in 1867 and established himself as a journalist. Following a visit to Germany, he wrote the two books mentioned by James which became instantaneous best sellers, both expressions (as James accurately puts it) of 'Teutophobia'': *Voyage au Pays des Milliards* (1875) and *Les Prussiens en Allemagne* (1876).

[9] The "gentleman of Germanic sympathies" of whom James spoke was probably Baron Holstein, secretary of the German Embassy, with whom James dined on a number of occasions during his winter in Paris and whom he described in a letter home as "one of the most acute and intelligent men I have ever met."

Letter 11

[1] Alexandre Gabriel Decamps (1803–1860), landscape and genre painter, became one of the leaders of the modern French Romantic school. In 1827, traveling to Greece, Constantinople, and Asia Minor, he formed a lasting predilection for oriental subjects, which he treated with consummate power and skill. The directions taken by the evolution of modern

painting have resulted in an undervaluing of Decamps' technical mastery, the subjects through which he expressed himself no longer arousing wide artistic interest.

² Pierre-Étienne Rousseau (1812–1867), founder of the modern French school of landscape painting, was noted especially for his ability to render atmospheric effects.

³ Prosper-Georges-Antoine Marilhat (1811–1847) traveled in Syria, Palestine, and Egypt, finding his subjects in the caravans and oases of the desert and in the streets of oriental villages. In Cairo, he painted portraits, notably that of Mehemet-Ali. He had achieved great fame by the time of his premature death.

⁴ The problem of the Khedive shares was much in the headlines at this time. The Khedive, Ismail Pasha, a semi-independent ruler in Egypt, had been fantastically reckless in his personal and state expenses, and in thirteen years had increased the national debt from about £3,000,000 to £100,-000,000. Most of his money had been derived from bonds sold chiefly to French and English investors. He replaced his English adviser, Charles Gordon, by an incapable Egyptian, and both the Sudan and Egypt were rapidly going bankrupt. In 1876 the Khedive suspended payment of debts and France insisted on a commission which would receive directly a part of the national income for the benefit of bondholders without going through the hands of corrupt officials. The British eventually joined the French in this commission.

⁵ Jacques Raymond Brascassat (1804–1867) preceded Rosa Bonheur (1822–1899) in reviving the painting of animals, to which he devoted himself almost exclusively after 1831. He became a vogue with rich collectors but was never so well known as Rosa Bonheur, whose fame was so great that during the Franco-Prussian War her studio and residence were respected by special order of the Crown Prince of Prussia.

⁶ Paul Potter (1625–1654), early Dutch animal painter,

was noted for the accuracy and objectivity of his paintings of horses and cattle.

[7] Ernest Baillet was the pupil of Saunier rather than Breton. He was born in Brest. He exhibited in salons from 1877 to 1897, painting mostly the landscapes and peasants of Brittany.

[8] Jean Boldini (1842–1931), an artist who began his study in Florence and who settled in Paris around 1872, was at this time beginning a notable career. Most of his honors (two grand prizes at the International Expositions of 1889 and 1900, and the Legion of Honor) still lay before him. He was primarily a portrait painter, whose work is distinguished for the feeling of intensity of life created in his characters.

[9] Any book by Ernest Renan (1823–1892) was an event of the first literary importance on the Parisian scene. Renan had won the Prix Volney in 1847 (at the age of twenty-four) for his general history of semitic languages. In the years following he undertook the study of the relation of the intellectual elite to democracy, becoming the philosopher to articulate most successfully the ideal of the intellectual life. From 1857 to 1859 he published the essays which won him renown as a stylist. In 1860 he went on a mission to Phoenicia and Syria, out of which came his various biblical studies. The Franco-Prussian War revived his interest in French political problems, but his work of the 1870's was marred, as James notes, by disillusionment and excessive irony.

[10] The salon of Marie de Flavigny, Countess d'Agoult (1805–1876), had been the rendezvous of the celebrities of her time. Her liaison with Franz Liszt was notorious. She wrote historical and philosophical works, expressing her ideas with forthrightness and energy.

[11] Louise Revoil Colet (1810–1876) wrote chiefly poetry, but was better known for her beauty and her amours with Cousin, Villemain, Musset, and, above all, Flaubert. *Lui,* her

novel about Musset, was published in 1859. George Sand's
Lui et Elle came out in the same year.

LETTER 12

[1] This letter was revised by James and reprinted in *Portraits of Places,* 1883.

[2] General Marceau of the First Republic was François Marceau Desgraviers (1769–1796).

LETTER 13

[1] "Cham" was the pseudonym of Amédée de Noé (1819–1879), prolific and spirited cartoonist. He published a number of albums in which the history of the ideas, manners, politics, art, and literature of the preceding era were rendered "avec une légère myopie conservatrice."

Honoré Daumier (1808–1879), the greatest of all French caricaturists, raised this medium to the level of art.

[2] The second exhibition of the Impressionists comprised 252 paintings, pastels, water colors, drawings, and etchings by 20 exhibitors. Degas was represented by 24 works; Monet 18; Berthe Morisot 17, and Renoir 15. The French press was violent in its denunciation of the exhibit. Albert Wolff of *Le Figaro* said: "It is a frightening spectacle of human vanity gone astray to the point of madness."

The enlightened patronage of Durand-Ruel, who supplied moral as well as financial support, resulted in most of the Impressionists' shunning the Salon, from which they would doubtless have been rejected in any case. Public disapproval of their art usually took the form (as with James) of finding their subjects "ugly," but the actual basis of Impressionist experimentation was, in reality, essentially technical: they were interested in the study of light, using a commalike brush stroke to create more of nature—the sunny air, the character of the hour, etc. Zola, interestingly enough, called them naturalists for this reason. The definition given by one of Renoir's friends at this time, "treating a subject in terms of its tone and not of the subject itself," perhaps best describes their purposes.

It is interesting that James, who himself came to be increasingly absorbed by "tone" (in so far as this is represented in fiction through isolation of point of view), should have failed to grasp the relationship between the subject matter of the Impressionists and their manner of rendering it. He did eventually, however, make his peace with the "intransigents." In a notable passage in *The American Scene,* describing a visit in 1904 to a Connecticut house hung with "wondrous examples of Manet, Degas, of Claude Monet, of Whistler . . ." James proclaimed that "no proof of the sovereign power of art could have been . . . sharper. It made everything else shrivel and fade: it was like the sudden trill of the nightingale. . . ."

³ The opening of *Jeanne d'Arc* by Auguste Mermet (1810–1889) was on April 5, 1876, and is memorable as the first new work to be produced in the new Paris Opera House. (Marie) Gabrielle Krauss (1842–1906) made her debut in Paris at the Théâtre Italien in *Il Trovatore,* April 6, 1867. She accepted an engagement at the Paris Opera in 1874, where she made her debut in *La Juive* in 1875. In time she became as great an actress as singer; the French called her "La Rachel Chantant."

⁴ Charles Augustin Sainte-Beuve (1804–1869) first won notice as literary critic of *Le Globe.* A favorable article on Victor Hugo brought him into close friendship and literary association with the leader of the French Romantic move-

ment. In 1828 he published his comprehensive study of the poets of the Pléiade, the ancestors of the Romantic poets. He also published poetry and romantic fiction of his own. In 1837 he went to Switzerland and began his monumental study of the Jansenist movement. Appointed to the chair of literature at the University of Liége, in Belgium, he undertook a study of Chateaubriand which aroused wide controversy. His various articles dealing with significant contemporary and earlier writers solidly established him as a literary critic. These essays were collected under the titles: *Critiques et Portraits Littéraires, Portraits Littéraires, Portraits Contemporains, Causeries du Lundi,* and *Nouveaux Lundis.*

Sainte-Beuve was a founder of modern literary criticism, developing a historical approach (set forth as a doctrine in his article on Chateaubriand in 1862) in which the literary work must not be considered apart from the writer and in which careful research into biography is therefore essential. The various posthumous volumes which were appearing were collections of Sainte-Beuve's articles for various Parisian papers.

[5] James's attitude toward the "posthumous rummaging" of table drawers echoes his comments on the publication of Hawthorne's notebooks, when he wondered about "the proper limits of curiosity" and observed that artists "will be likely to take alarm, empty their table-drawers, and level the approaches to their privacy. The critics, psychologists, and gossip-mongers may then glean amid the stubble."

[6] Émile Zola (1840–1902) was to found the naturalist school of fiction and to write his Rougon-Macquart series (1871–1893), a group of twenty novels which traces the "natural" and social history of a family under the Second Empire. Although James continued to have reservations about him, he ultimately came to have great respect for his achievement. The identification of Zola with Flaubert (1821–1880) probably resulted from James's meeting Zola in Flaubert's

circle. It also reflects the controversy over *Madame Bovary* (1856–1857), for which Flaubert had been accused (and acquitted) of immorality. The book was hailed as a masterpiece of realism. By 1876 Flaubert had published his revised versions of *L'Éducation Sentimentale* and *La Tentation de St. Antoine*, but James's reaction to Flaubert was as much in terms of his realism as of his stylistic innovations.

LETTER 14

[1] The artists viewed by James in this review of the Salon of 1876 were: Paul Gustave Doré (1833–1883), history painter and designer; Xavier Alphonse Monchablon (1835–1907), history and portrait painter, winner of the Grand Prix de Rome in 1863; Jean Baptiste Philippe Émile Bin (1825–1897), history painter and decorator of public and private buildings; Paul Joseph Blanc (1846–1905), genre painter; Valerico Lacetti (1836–1909), history and genre painter; Joseph Noel Sylvestre (1847–1926), history, genre, and portrait painter, winner of the Prize of the Salon of 1876; Albert Aublet (1851–1937(?)); Jean Baptiste Édouard Detaille (1848–1912), one of the most popular contemporary painters; Michel Munkacsy (Michael Lieb) (1844–1909), history, genre, and portrait painter; and Jules Bastien-Lepage (1848–1884), who had won universal approbation the year previously for his "Annunciation."

LETTER 15

[1] The artists whose works James notes here were: Émile-Auguste Carolus-Duran (1838–1917), portrait painter and sculptor; Paul Baudry (1828–1886) (see Letter 1); Alexan-

dre Cabanel (1824–1889), whose reputation had been made
in 1845 with his tableau, "Jésus dans le Prétoire"; Charles
Chaplin (1825–1891), noted for his charming paintings of
young girls; Édouard Jacquemart (née Nélie André) (1841–
1912), noted for her portraits of leaders in society and
politics, winner of medals at the Salons of 1868, 1869,
and 1870; Alexei Charlamoff (also spelled Harlamoff) (1842–
(?)), product of the Academy of Beaux Arts in Petersburg
and student of Bonnant in Paris; George Clarin (1843–
1919), whose portrait of Sarah Bernhardt in this Salon made
a great sensation; Louise Abbéma (1858–1927), young pupil
of Chaplin and Carolus-Duran, whose portrait of Sarah
Bernhardt also created a tremendous impression at the Salon;
Léon-Joseph Bonnant (1834–1923), famous for his portraits
of such notables as Hugo, Thiers, Renan, Félix Faure, and
winner of the medal of the Salon of 1869; Antoine Vollon
(1833–1900), regarded as one of the *petits maîtres* in landscape painting and particularly relished by James; William
Adolphe Bouguereau (1825–1905), one of the most prolific
French painters, whose strenuous schedule of output led to a
superficiality which James found "perverse"; Jehan Georges
Vibert (1840–1902), whose specialty was the depiction of
the trivial lapses of the clergy, humorously viewed; Karl-
Pierre Daubigny (1846–1885), one of the most charming
landscapists of this period; François-Louis Français (1814–
1897), famous landscapist, whose "Le Miroir de Scey" and
"Portrait of M.B." were shown at this Salon; Joseph Chelmonski (1850–1914), Russian landscapist, who submitted two
scenes of the Ukraine to this Salon and whom James believed
to have followed the famous Dutch landscapist Salomon van
Ruysdael (1600–1670); Edward Harrison May (1824–1887),
pupil of Huntington in New York and of Couture in Paris;
Henry Bacon (1839–1912), born in Massachusetts, pupil of
Cabanel and Frère; Edgar Melville Ward (1839–1915), born

Notes

in Ohio, pupil of Cabanel; Frederic Arthur Bridgman (1847–(?)), from New York, pupil of Gérôme; Paul Dubois (1829–1905), the distinguished sculptor of the 1860's and 1870's, who won the medal of honor in the Salon of 1867 and whose figures were admired for their representation of ideal beauty; and Sarah Bernhardt (1844–1923), the actress, who had studied sculpture with Gustave Doré and who won honorable mention for her work in this exhibit.

LETTER 16

[1] Renan's *Dialogues Philosophiques*, written in 1871, reveals a disenchanted temper, but the struggles of democratic France for survival roused Renan to take a more affirmative attitude in later works.

[2] Jules Michelet, the historian, died on February 9, 1874. He was first buried at Hyères, according to his last wishes expressed to his wife on his deathbed, but the civil tribunal of Seine ordered (in August 1875) that his body be exhumed and given a more appropriate final resting place in Paris. He was buried in the cemetery d'Est May 17, 1876.

[3] Paul-Armand Challemel-Lacour (1827–1896), philosopher and politician, friend of Gambetta and Prefect of Rhône in 1870.

[4] Gabriel Paul d'Haussonville (1843–1924), politician and prolific writer on social and literary subjects, published in 1875 the life of Sainte-Beuve to which James alludes. He was elected to the Academy in 1888.

[5] Germaine de Staël (1766–1817) was born Anne Louise Germaine Necker and married a Swedish diplomat, Baron Staël-Holstein. Her salon and her unconventional love affairs were famous. Her novel *Corinne* (1807) was widely read. Her principal work was *De l'Allemagne* (1811), which con-

tributed to the spread of German romanticism. Her opposition
to Napoleon caused her exile from Paris to Switzerland.

⁶ Sully-Prudhomme (René François Armand) (1839–1907),
poet. He was elected member of the Academy in 1881 and
won the Nobel Prize in 1901.

⁷ The Salon of the Refusés, 1876, included the work of those
Impressionists who had submitted paintings to the Salon and
had been rejected. Among these, but unmentioned by James,
was Manet's "Artist, Portrait of Marcellin Desbourtier."

⁸ James Fairman, Scottish-American landscape painter
(1826–1904), traveled to Europe in 1871 and remained
abroad for ten years but exhibited without success.

LETTER 17

¹ Ximènes Doudan (1800–1872) served as secretary to Victor de Broglie, Minister of Education. The correspondence of
Doudan was published under the title *Mélanges et Lettres de
Doudan,* 1876. James speaks of having "marked a great many
passages for quotation," and the volumes, preserved in Henry
James's library up to the time of its dispersal give proof of
this.

² The "dark clouds in the East" is a reference to events in
Bosnia and Herzegovina, which led to a new Russo-Turkish
War, 1877–1878.

³ Jean Baptiste Dumas (1800–1884) replaced the historian
François Guizot, who died in 1874.

⁴ At the "feast of vocalism" represented by Verdi's *Aïda*
and *Requiem,* James heard: Rosine Stoltz (1815–1903),
mezzo-soprano; Maria Waldmann (1844–1920), Austrian
mezzo-soprano, who had become famous as Amneris in the
first Italian performance of *Aïda* and for whom Verdi subsequently wrote the mezzo-soprano part in the *Requiem;* Paolo

Medini (1831–1911), who sang leading roles in such operas as *Norma, Don Carlos,* and *Rigoletto;* and Angelo Masini (1844–1926), the first of the younger tenors of Italy.

[5] James had spoken about George Sand that winter with Turgenev and Flaubert.

LETTER 18

[1] George Sand (Aurore Lucille Dupin) (1804–1876). This letter was reprinted in *French Poets and Novelists,* 1878. James wrote at least seven papers and reviews of the work of George Sand, the three most important being collected in *Notes on Novelists* (1914).

LETTER 19

[1] This account of Rouen was revised and reprinted in *Portraits of Places,* 1883.

[2] The old center of Rouen was destroyed in World War II, particularly in 1944 in the battle for the Seine crossings. The cathedral (1202–20), which has three very beautiful towers, an impressive nave, and a choir, transepts, and portals of great distinction, was severely damaged, especially on the south side. St. Ouen Church (1318–39), with a fine choir, escaped any considerable war damage.

[3] James incorrectly identifies one of the two cardinals. George II d'Amboise (1488–1550), nephew of George I d'Amboise (1460–1510), was attached to the Duke of Orléans, minister and counselor of Louis XII.

LETTER 20

[1] This letter was revised and reprinted in *Portraits of Places,* 1883.

[2] Alphonse Karr (1808–1890), "celebrity" of Étretat, was a writer of romantic novels.

[3] Offenbach had retired to Étretat after a fabulously successful career. James's reference to his "not shaking his legs and making play with his eyes" refers to the gestures of performers in his operettas, especially the movements of the *can-can.*

[4] Mlle. X, the actress of the Palais Royal, was probably Céline Chaumont, to whom James had referred in some of his earlier letters.

INDEX